EvangeLife: A Guide to Life-style Evangelism

EvangeLife:
A Guide to Life-style Evangelism

DAN R. CRAWFORD

BROADMAN PRESS
Nashville, Tennessee

4262-47
ISBN: 0-8054-6247-3

Dewey Decimal Classification: 248.5
Subject Headings: WITNESSING // CHRISTIAN LIFE
Library of Congress Catalog Card Number: 84-1805
Printed in the United States of America

Library of Congress Cataloging in Publication Data

Crawford, Dan R., 1941-
  EvangeLife, a guide to life-style evangelism.

  Bibliography: p.
  1. Evangelistic work. 2. Witness bearing
(Christianity) 3. Christian life—Baptist authors.
I. Title. II. Title: Life-style evangelism.
BV3793.C67 1984   248.4'861   84-1805
ISBN 0-8054-6247-3 (pbk.)

Unless otherwise indicated, Scripture quotations are from the *New American Standard Bible.* Copyright © The Lockman Foundation, 1960, 1962, 1963, 1968, 1971, 1972, 1973, 1975, 1977. Used by permission.

Scripture quotations marked (GNB) are from the *Good News Bible,* the Bible in Today's English Version. Old Testament: Copyright © American Bible Society 1976; New Testament: Copyright © American Bible Society 1966, 1971, 1976. Used by permission.

Scripture quotations marked (KJV) are from the King James Version of the Bible.

Scripture quotations marked (NEB) are from *The New English Bible.* Copyright © The Delegates of the Oxford University Press and the Syndics of the Cambridge University Press, 1961, 1970. Reprinted by permission.

Scripture quotations marked (NIV) are from the HOLY BIBLE *New International Version,* copyright © 1978, New York Bible Society. Used by permission.

Scripture quotations marked (Phillips) are reprinted with permission of Macmillan Publishing Co., Inc. from J. B. Phillips: The New Testament in Modern English, Revised Edition. © J. B. Phillips 1958, 1960, 1972.

To my parents, Inez and Edwin Crawford, forty-five years in the ministry and still serving and to the memories of A. L. Gilliam, my grandfather, and Chet Reames, my friend, both of whom believed in me and were not afraid to express it

Acknowledgments

Long before these ideas were ever put into print, two Baptist congregations and students of three Baptist Student Unions faithfully heard, gently challenged, and hopefully applied many of these ideas. Thanks to the people of the Robinson Springs Baptist Church, DeLeon, Texas; the Pisgah Baptist Church, Frankston, Texas; the Baptist Student Union of Pan American University, Edinburg, Texas; the Baptist Student Union of East Texas State University, Commerce, Texas; and the Baptist Student Union of the University of Texas, Austin, Texas, for their love and help to their pastor and director.

No man writes new truth, only new insight into truth, all of which comes from God, much of which comes through persons. We have all been taught by committed teachers. I have been especially blessed to have had many helpful teachers both in the classroom and in various seminars and workshops. From these teachers much of the insight in this book finds its human origin. Thanks go to the "special" teachers, listed in the order in which I met them:

Mrs. Myrle Acton who kept telling a class of sixth graders at West University Elementary School in Houston, Texas, that there was potential greatness in our class. I believed her.

Miss Janie Belle Baten, English teacher, Reagan High School, Houston, Texas, who forced me to memorize.

Dr. A. J. Quinn, professor of religious education at Howard Payne University, Brownwood, Texas, who taught me it was OK to be human.

Drs. Cal Guy, David Garland, Virtus Gideon, Roy Fish, James Eaves, and *Justice Anderson,* Southwestern Baptist Theological Seminary professors who taught me not only through their lectures but also through their lives.

Drs. Ralph Neighbor, Jr., Jack Stanton, C. Peter Wagner, and *D. James Kennedy* who in workshops and seminars added fresh insight into my continuing education.

Joyce Ashcraft, Charles Baker, James W. Hatley, W. F. Howard, and *Browning Ware* who in the classroom of life's interaction have taught me much.

The materials in this book were first developed as *EvangeLife: A Seminar in Lifestyle Evangelism*—with three editions: College Adult Edition, Single Adult Edition, and Married Adult Edition. Thanks are expressed to the following groups for assisting me in the field testing of the seminar materials and thus eventually making the book more applicable to life:

- Baptist Student Union, University of Mary Hardin-Baylor (Texas);
- San Francisco Mandarin Baptist Church, San Francisco, California;
- Baptist Student Ministries, Idaho State University;
- Baptist Campus Ministry, Baptist College of Charleston (South Carolina);
- Baptist Student Union, Georgia Tech (Atlanta, Georgia);
- Baptist Student Union, Missouri University;
- Park Cities Baptist Church, Dallas, Texas;
- Calvary Baptist Church, Aberdeen, New Jersey;
- Baptist Campus Ministry, University of Maryland;
- Columbia Baptist Church, Falls Church, Virginia;
- University Baptist Church, Coral Gables, Florida;
- Two Rivers Baptist Church, Nashville, Tennessee;
- First Baptist Church, Lilburn, Georgia;
- Baptist Student Union, Auburn, University (Alabama);
- Baptist Student Union, University of Southwestern Louisiana;
- Wieuca Road Baptist Church, Atlanta, Georgia;
- Baptist Student Union, Hawaii Baptist Convention;
- Baptist Student Union, California Baptist College;
- Metro Baptist Church, New York, New York;
- Clay-Platte Baptist Association, Kansas City, Missouri;
- Second Baptist Church, Marion, Illinois;

- Evangelism Department, Virginia Baptist General Board;
- First Baptist Church, Dallas, Texas;
- Naperville Baptist Church, Naperville, Illinois;
- Parkway Baptist Church, Saint Louis, Missouri;
- Atlanta Baptist Association, Atlanta, Georgia;
- First Baptist Church, Tallahassee, Florida;
- Tarrant Baptist Association, Fort Worth, Texas;
- Southwestern Baptist Theological Seminary, Fort Worth, Texas;
- Riverside Baptist Church, Denver, Colorado;
- Tampa Bay Baptist Association, Tampa, Florida;

A final thanks to my wife, Joanne, and my children, Danna Ruth and James Edwin, and to the staff and consultants of the Southern Baptist Home Mission Board, Evangelism Section. These people believed in this project and made various contributions all of which were helpful and appreciated.

Preface

Why Another Book on Evangelism?

Taking notes on the sermon and discussing our favorite idea or quote has proven to be a very positive experience for our family, not to mention being much better than what we used to do on the way home from church. In a recent sermon, our pastor, Truett Gannon, made reference to certain aspects of the Christian life-style and illustrated by telling of a child and his imaginary friend. Then he said, "It's OK for children to see what is not there, but it is a sin for adults to not see what is there."

This idea brought about a discussion on the way home from church that led Danna, our daughter who is blossoming into her teenage years with the typical peer pressures, to confess a recent experience where she had deceived a friend. She wanted to justify her actions on the basis that it was all right for "children to see what is not there." As I was trying to share with Danna what the pastor meant by that statement as well as what was wrong with deceiving friends, I said, *"My* Bible (with strong emphasis on the word *my*) tells me its wrong to deceive another person."

Danna's younger brother, James, silent up until now, burst forth in response to my statement with, "Don't they all?"

Danna's discussion was temporarily interrupted as I explained to James that, yes, all Bibles do say the same thing but that I was trying to help Danna see that *her* Bible condemned deceitful practices. Somehow I felt that all my theological training was inadequate to deal with the issues in the car that Sunday. As I tried to answer one child, I created a much larger problem for the other child.

What does all of this have to do with another book on evangelism?

Granted, all Bibles do say the same thing. But people differ greatly as to their understanding and application of that sameness. The purpose of this book on evangelism is to motivate, challenge, and equip you in life-style evangelism. That, on the surface, makes it no different from other books. The difference is: this is my understanding and application of the truths of the Bible—my Bible and yours.

It is my prayer that, as you read these pages, you will not just look for answers in my words. Rather, as you evaluate and experiment with these principles, I hope you will find answers in your own experience and "as you go" you will be a more effective witness for Jesus Christ.

Contents

1

The Importance of EvangeLife

An Introduction

Hungry? Man! Was I ever hungry! The day had started so fast there was no time for breakfast. The further into the day I went, the more the work load increased. Lunch was bypassed in favor of attempting to catch up with my "To Do" list. Shortly after lunchtime, I had to leave town for a speaking engagement at Auburn University. As I drove down the interstate from Atlanta to Auburn, my stomach began to send signals to my brain that it feared my throat had been cut. About that time I saw a sign—"Truck Stop/Food"—and I knew it was time for breakfast/brunch/lunch.

I was halfway through my meal when I realized that I was one of only two customers in the restaurant. As the waitress, who was acting as busy as if it were rush hour, passed by the table of my fellow diner he exclaimed, "Slow down, Honey, before you kill yourself!" Her instant reply was, "Moving fast is the only thing that keeps me alive . . ." Several minutes later as she passed by the trucker's table again she continued her sentence as if there had been no time lapse, "that and the grace of God." In the next fifteen minutes, I watched this truck-stop waitress pass the trucker's table repeatedly, often stopping, sharing with him in bits and pieces, the story of her life and how God had changed her and given her meaning and purpose. As the trucker left the restaurant, I heard the waitress say, "Yes, Sir! Ruth and Jesus have got a good thing going."

When Jesus gave the Great Commission to his disciples, he included only one imperative: "make disciples." Both "baptizing" and "teaching" are what we know as participles, and the word *go* not being an imperative might better be translated "as you go" since Jesus assumed that his disciples would go. Thus the Great Commission might well be translated, "As you go, make disciples of all people, baptizing them in the name of the Father and the Son and the Holy Spirit, teaching them to observe all that I have commanded you; and remember that I will be with you even to the end of the age" (Matt. 28:19-20).

Life-style evangelism is making disciples "as you go." Ruth, the truck-stop waitress, is a perfect example of one bearing witness and sharing testimony as she went about. The purpose of this book is to guide you in life-style evangelism "as you go." The positive response of many non-Christians to the gospel of Jesus Christ awaits the positive living out of the Christian life on the part of Christians. An attempt to "make disciples" for Jesus Christ "as you go" begins with a look at the facts.

Importance of the Facts

While Christians go about, the majority of the world goes to hell. In 1969 the population of the world was 29 percent Christian according to *The World Almanac, 1970.*[1] By the year 1982, according to the same source of information, that percentage had decreased to 22.2 percent with 43 percent of the world's population not affiliated with any major religion.[2] At that rate of decrease and the projected rate of world population increase, by the year 2000 the world will be approximately 3 percent Christian.

When I was young, "Go to hell" was a slang phrase, and we were told not to say it. Today it is the life-style of so many people that we cannot ignore it. We Christians are busy about many things, most of them good, but the world misses the best thing. May we not have to respond to God as another servant responded to another king, "While your servant was busy here and there, the man disappeared" (1 Kings 20:40, NIV). We have tried many methods of communicating the gospel to the non-Christians.

One of the earliest methods of communicating the gospel to non-Christians was what I will call the come-and-hear method. This method says if we can get the non-Christian to *come* to where the gospel is being presented, he or she will *hear,* and his or her chances of becoming a Christian will be increased. Jesus used this method among others. As he taught in the public places, the people came and heard and many believed. The only thing wrong with the method is recent surveys have shown the majority of people do not choose to go to places where the gospel is being presented. We must conclude that this method alone will not reverse the fact that the world is growing increasingly non-Christian.

Another method of communicating the gospel to non-Christians is what I will call the go-and-tell method. It is based on the fact that Christ did not command the world to *come* to the church and *hear* but rather commanded the church to *go* to the world and *tell.* Even with our best efforts, the vast majority of Christian churches have little or no witness training as a part of their church programs. Southern Baptists, among others, have taken the task of going and telling seriously. But as reported from their 1979 Uniform Church Letter, only 12.3 percent of all Southern Baptist churches had witness training events in their church programs during 1979. That means 87.7 percent of Southern Baptist churches reported having no witness training in an entire church year.[3] We must conclude that this method alone will not reverse the fact that the world is growing increasingly non-Christian.

This book proposes a go-and-live method of communicating the gospel to non-Christians. In a sense, go-and-live evangelism involves aspects of both the come-and-hear and the go-and-tell methods. It maintains that evangelism should be your entire life-style as a Christian rather than a section of your life.

Often I have an early flight to a speaking engagement and will leave my house quite early. On these mornings, the only part of the newspaper I am interested in is the sports news. If I can get the ball scores early, I will be content to wait until I get where I am going to read the rest of the news. So on mornings when I have early departures, I simply slip the sports section out of the paper as it lays on my driveway, roll the rest of the paper back into a neat package, and leave it for the family to read. Never yet have I missed a strategic score because it was placed in the classified ads or on the society page. The sports news is always in the sports section, with the rare exception when it makes front-page news. The point is that sports is a section of the newspaper, not the entire paper. I hope your life is not like that. I hope evangelism is not just a section of your life but rather your life-style. That's what EvangeLife means.

The Importance of Definitions

In a study of life-style evangelism, it will be well to define some terms beginning with the word *evangelism*. *Evangel* means "good news" or "good message" or "good tidings." *Ism* means "doing" that which precedes it. Thus, *Evangelism* means "doing the good news." Even though the word *evangelism* does not appear in the Bible, both Philip (Acts 21:8) and Timothy (2 Tim. 4:5) were related to the word *evangelist,* and Paul described "evangelists" as one of the spiritual gifts that God has given to the church (Eph. 4:11).

The verb form of "evangelism" is the word *euaggelizo* and appears many times in the New Testament. Used in its verb form, *euaggelizo* means to share or proclaim or gossip the good news. The angels acting as "evangelists" were said to have "evangelized" when they brought "good news of great joy" (Luke 2:10, NIV) to all people at the birth of Jesus Christ. By its frequent use of the verb form of "evangelism," the New Testament seems to stress the activity of the good news, or "doing" the good news.

EvangeLife is a coined word which stands for "living the good news." Since evangelism means "doing the good news," EvangeLife could mean "living" the good news. Thus we have coined a new word for life-style evangelism. Someone has said that communication is a comprehensive process involving the printed word (7 percent), voice tone (38 percent) and life-style (55 percent).[4] If this is true, there is a need for greater emphasis on the life-style as a means of evangelizing.

Life-style evangelism is your life lived out in Jesus' style. You are not called to live out Jesus' life in his style, for that would be an attempt to imitate the perfect which would be impossible. You are not called to live out your life in your own style, for that would be an attempt to disregard the claims of Christ on your life. You are called to live out his life in your style, with your God-given personality and with your human limitations. Perhaps this is what Paul meant when he said, "I have been crucified with Christ and I no longer live, but Christ lives *in me*" (Gal. 2:20, NIV, *verbal witness + lifestyle witness*

Author's italics). Thus, the importance of life-style evangelism as a means of communicating the good news of Jesus Christ.

The Importance of Life-style Evangelism

We have very subtly separated two concepts that ought not be separated. I have often heard someone say, "I can't talk about Jesus Christ, but my life is my witness." This concept proposes that life-style witnessing can stand apart from verbal witnessing. On the other hand, I have known a few people who do a great job of verbalizing the good news of Jesus Christ, but their life-styles leave much to be desired. Their lives do not even come close to living up to the verbalized truth. This concept proposes that verbal witness is sufficient apart from life-style witness. Let me attempt to put these two concepts—verbal witness and life-style witness— together.

Let us look first at evangelism as verbal witness. Through the years, I have observed that verbal witness apart from a committed Christian lifestyle will be short lived. It is like an injection that wears off after a while. When the level of commitment drops to a certain point, the verbalization ceases. The amount of verbal witness is directly related to the level of spiritual commitment. Obviously, this works well when the spiritual commitment level is high, but most of us do not live on a consistent spiritual "high."

The church wasn't very large, but I wasn't much of a preacher. My excuse was inexperience—it was my first attempt at being a pastor. Their excuse was few people—the community sat at the intersection of two farm roads and consisted of a few houses, a Baptist church, a Methodist church, an outdoor tabernacle, a cemetery, and a Fina Service Station which sold groceries, fertilizer, real estate, and several other things in addition to gasoline and oil. Early in the summer, one of the deacons told me to get an evangelist for the August revival. I didn't know that we were scheduled to have an August revival, but I was informed, "We always have a revival the third week in August." I was also told to appoint a committee to clean out the tabernacle. That's when I discovered, "We always have the revival under the tabernacle." I'm not sure what I expected, but on the first night the place was packed. When the invitation was given, many came forward to rededicate their lives and made very bold commitments as to what they planned to do for the Lord in the future. My excitement over the "revival" lasted about one week longer than their commitment. By September everything was back to "normal," and the world was again turning at the Fina Station. The verbal commitments were not backed up by life-style commitments and were thus short lived. I saw similar results in two other churches that I served as pastor. It was not unique to churches.

In my fifteen years of campus ministry, I saw short-lived verbalization not backed up by life-style commitment. I was privileged to serve as a campus minister on three campuses that were very different from each other. Pan American University was largely Hispanic with students who still maintained strong ties to home and church. East Texas State University was a teachers college that grew up and was rather evenly populated with students from the metropolitan area of Dallas, Texas, and students from such small towns as Ladonia, Honey Grove, Sulphur Bluff, and Frog Knot. By 4:00 PM on Friday the campus was deserted, and the last one to leave turned out the light. The University of Texas was a major university with fifty thousand students, one of each kind. On these diverse campuses, I found a similar response. We could schedule an evangelistic emphasis, and the students involved in our ministry got excited, witnessed to other students, and made bold commitments. Halfway through the next exam week, it was all over. Again, verbalization ceased with the drop in spiritual commitment. Unless the commitment is one that is deep enough to involve a change of life-style, the verbalization will be short lived and will return only as the spiritual level rises again. To be fair, I want to say that in every place I have served, I have found those with deep, abiding commitments to Jesus Christ that resulted in consistent verbalizing of their faith. To be honest, I want to say those people were always in the minority. Let's look at the other concept of evangelism.

Not only is evangelism seen as verbal witness but it is also seen as life-style witness. The non-Christian has the right to validate what you say about your Christian experience by examining your life-style. If you are not living it, chances are they won't want it. In a recent seminar, I was challenged on this point. A former pastor who had been through a divorce and as a result resigned his church responded to me, "You just don't understand. I'm still trying to put the pieces of my life back together, and you say the non-Christian has the right to validate something by my life-style?" My response was that I did not say the non-Christian has the right to validate the gospel by our life-styles, Jesus has already done that. The non-Christian does have the right to expect from the Christian the highest level of integrity. If you are struggling with your life, how many non-Christians are in the same condition? Tell them of your struggles, then tell them about your outside resource, Jesus Christ. If you are not experiencing the "abundant life," don't go around talking to people about it as though you were. Paul said he had every right to boast but refrained "so that no one may credit me with more than he sees in me or hears from me" (2 Cor. 12:6). Go ahead and verbalize what is happening in your life, but be sure to do it in integrity, and be sure to point non-Christians to Jesus Christ as the resource that helps you cope with what is happening.

My friend Jim Ulrich sells Oldsmobiles. We have been friends since we were in our early teenage years. We lived two blocks apart. We played baseball and basketball together. We double-dated together. We car pooled to school together. He served as a groomsman in my wedding. We are close friends. After returning from Vietnam, Jim went to work for his father-in-law selling Oldsmobiles. Upon the death of his father-in-law, he became owner-president of Ulrich Oldsmobile in Crockett, Texas. I buy Oldsmobiles from Jim Ulrich. I have bought more than one Olds from him completely on his word, with very little investigation. I would not do that with someone I do not know. But I know Jim Ulrich. I trust Jim Ulrich. And do you know what else? Jim Ulrich drives Oldsmobiles. He believes they are the best cars on the road. Because of my relationship with him, I buy what he sells. The day I walk on the lot of Ulrich Oldsmobile and find Jim driving a Ford, I'm through buying Oldsmobiles from him. I buy cars from Jim Ulrich because his life-style of driving Oldsmobiles and his verbalization of selling Oldsmobiles are consistent with each other. He is a man of integrity. His verbalization matches his life-style. That's the kind of witness I want to be and the kind I want you to be. So let's put the two concepts together.

Evangelism must not be seen as either/or but as both/and. Evangelism is not either verbal witness or life-style witness. Evangelism is both verbal witness and life-style witness. It is my opinion that the term *life-style witness* communicates both concepts better than the term *verbal witness.* Life-style evangelism, EvangeLife, includes both verbal and life-style witness. Thus, it is of utmost importance in the Christian life.

One thing more: the work of evangelism must be seen as the recipient of God's blessing. Several years ago, I went through a well-known course in evangelism training. I must confess that my reason for being there was to observe from a critical standpoint rather than to learn. But this method had become so popular that I felt I needed to learn it firsthand, from the man who wrote the materials. In the first session, after handing out a huge notebook, the leader began to teach, and I began to write in the margins of my notebook. All of my writing was negative. I wrote, "This won't work," and "This is not practical," and "I don't agree with this," and other such statements in the first third of my seminar notebook.

We were then told that it was time to "go witnessing." In other words, we were going to try out our new method on a non-Christian. This bothered me because I had always felt that the non-Christian deserved more from me than being my "lab experiment," but I went. I was told not to talk because my teacher would do all the talking. That was fine with me since I was convinced the method would not work. We made three visits that night, and three persons accepted Christ as their personal Savior and Lord. Convicted of my attitude and convinced of the method's worth, I went back to my room and wrote in my seminar notebook about one third of the way through, "In spite of everything else I have written in this notebook, this method works." I had learned that, whether I accept it or not, God always blesses the sincere efforts of his people.

God will bless your sincere efforts to bear witness for him. In the Old Testament times, pillars on some of the buildings began to crack. In an attempt to patch up these cracks, some men used wax. Once the wax was in the cracks and polished it took on the appearance of marble, thus the cracks were covered up. Then it rained, and the rain washed out the wax from the cracks exposing the poor work of the repairmen. When the cracks were effectively patched with another substance, they began to call the new work *cine cera,* meaning "without wax." From their term *cine cera* we get our word *sincere* which means "honest, true, pure, genuine" or in other

Cine cera - "without wax"

words, "without wax." Regardless of the method you choose to use in bearing witness, God will bless your sincere effort. When the life-style undergirds the verbal and the verbal flows from the life-style, there is sincerity in our witness and God blesses.

My friend Howard Ramsey returned to the office with a story from a recent flight where the stewardess spilled part of a tray of food in his lap while attempting to pass it over to the man next to the window. Prior to the accident, Howard had bowed his head and said a silent blessing for his own food. With food in his lap and on his shirt, Howard very graciously helped the stewardess clean up her mess without any sign of anger or hostility whatsoever. When the ordeal was over, a man across the aisle said, "Hey, Buddy! You passed the test. I saw you pray, then I watched to see your reaction. You passed the test." The world is watching closer than we may realize. Many are waiting to see the Christian life lived out in someone's life. As you go, understand the importance of EvangeLife.

For Further Study

Aldrich, Joseph C. *Lifestyle Evangelism.* Portland: Multonomah Press, 1981.

Bailey, Waylon. *As You Go: Foundations for Evangelism.* New Orleans: Insight Press, 1981.

Chafin, Kenneth L. *The Reluctant Witness.* Nashville: Broadman Press, 1974.

Coleman, Robert E. *Evangelism in Perspective.* Harrisburg, Pa: Christian Publications, Inc. 1975.

DeVille, Jard. *The Psychology of Witnessing.* Waco: Word Books, 1980.

Howard, W. F. *Victorious Living.* Nashville: Convention Press, 1961.

Leavell, Landrum and Bryson, Harold. *Evangelism: Christ's Imperative Commission* (Revised Edition). Nashville: Broadman Press, 1979.

McDill, Wayne. *Making Friends for Christ.* Nashville: Broadman Press, 1979.

Miles, Delos. *Introduction to Evangelism.* Nashville: Broadman Press, 1983.

Moore, Waylon. *Multiplying Disciples.* Colorado Springs: Navpress, 1981.

Nouwen, Henri J. M. *Reaching Out.* Garden City, N.Y.: Doubleday Company, 1975.

Petersen, Jim. *Evangelism as a Lifestyle.* Colorado Springs: Navpress, 1980.

Pippert, Rebecca Manley. *Out of the Salt Shaker Into the World.* Downers Grove, Il: Inter Varsity Press, 1979.

Whitesell, Faris Daniel. *Basic New Testament Evangelism.* Grand Rapids, Mi.: Zondervan
    Publishing House, 1949.

Notes

1. "A Survey of Southern Baptist Progress," *The Quarterly Review,* July, August, September, 1970.
2. Ibid., p.79.
3. *Witnessing Through the Sunday School* (Nashville: The Sunday School Board of the Southern Baptist Convention, 1981), p.5.
4. Evangelism Explosion III International, Leadership Clinic Notes, 1980, p.84.

2

The Priority
of EvangeLife

Relationship to God

The best place to begin is at the beginning. Several years ago I took a course in modern Hebrew at the University of Texas. On the first day of class, the Jewish professor asked how many of us already knew the Hebrew alphabet. To my amazement, twenty of the twenty-three persons in the class raised their hands. I later discovered that all twenty were Jewish, and the other two Gentiles in the class were engaged to Jewish fiancés, providing for them private tutorship. The next statement from the professor was, "Very good! We will go on to vocabulary." Although I finished the semester with a *C* average, I am convinced that I could have done much better had the professor started where I was rather than beyond me.

Many witness training programs begin beyond the level of the participants. I have been through seminars and workshops that began with how to use a particular witnessing tract or how to effectively share a testimony. While these are of extreme importance, they are less than the utmost priority. For most Christians, witnessing methodology is less a need than witnessing motivation. The need is not so much to equip as it is to motivate, not so much to engraft technique as to implant vision. Witness begins with the Christian's relationship to God.

The Priority of Relationship to God

Amen!

One cannot share what one does not have. Thus to begin at any point other than the basic relationship to God is to begin beyond the beginning. The apostle Paul wrote, "I urge you therefore, brethren, by the mercies of God to present your bodies a living and holy sacrifice, acceptable to

God, which is your spiritual service of worship" (Rom. 12:1). There is a presentation in our relationship to God, a condition of our relationship to God, and a reason for our relationship to God.

Although we sing "All to Jesus I surrender, All to him I freely give," we content ourselves with giving only 10 percent. We have assumed that if we just give some of our money, attend church semiregularly, and treat folks fairly, we are in right relationship with God. Paul indicated that God does not want just 10 percent of our money or time nor even 99.44 percent, but he desires 100 percent—"present your bodies." That which is seen and represented by my "body" is all I really have to give God because it is all that is really mine to give. That is exactly what God wants from me—a presentation of my "body"—my all. But there are some conditions to that presentation.

Paul often leaned back on his Old Testament concept of God to explain a New Testament truth. In Old Testament days, one related to God through a sacrificial system—the killing of animals. The New Testament truth is God wants no more dead sacrifices but rather "living" sacrifices from us. In addition we are to be a "holy" sacrifice, that is, "set apart." We are "set apart" from the rest of the world, no longer to be like others, but now to be "acceptable to God." The thoroughness of our sacrificial presentation of self, although difficult, is based on good reason.

With so many demands on my life, why should I give all of myself to God? Paul indicated that it is my "spiritual service of worship" or, as the King James Version of the Bible says, "reasonable service." I give my all to God because it makes sense in a world where very little else makes sense. Giving all to God is "reasonable," logical, rational. In light of the fact that Jesus Christ, in the beginning with the Father, clothed this earth with flowers, grass, shrubs, and trees yet was allowed to hang naked on a cross, giving all to God is reasonable. In light of the fact that Jesus said, "I am the light of the world" (John 8:12) yet hung on the cross in midday darkness, giving all to God is reasonable. In light of the fact that Jesus claimed to give "living water" (John 4:10) yet cried out from the cross, "I am thirsty" (John 19:28), giving all to God is reasonable. In light of the fact that Jesus claimed, "All authority [power] has been given to Me in heaven and on earth" (Matt. 28:18) yet was allowed to hang powerless on the cross, giving all to God is reasonable. Relating to God begins with giving all to him. There are some basic ways of relating to God.

The Priority of Getting Back to the Basics

"What will you do if, in the upcoming championship game, you are entering the final few minutes and you are behind by a touchdown?" That question was asked by a news reporter to a former football coach. The answer was, "We will get back to the basics." One coach understood that games are not won or lost on fancy plays but on fundamental playing.

Never was I more surprised to see the basics than recently in Saint Petersburg, Florida. Since I had a spring engagement to speak in Tampa, Florida, I had arrived a few days early to watch the Saint Louis Cardinals baseball team in spring training. The Cardinals were the defending world series champions. For the first half hour I was there, the players did exercises, ran the bases, and played catch. After what seemed to be an eternity, the players took the field. Then to my utter amazement, I watched the World Series' most valuable player, catcher Darrell Porter, spend thirty minutes practicing picking a runner off first base on a pitchout from the pitcher. Before the morning was over, I watched the world champions practice bunting and sliding and other skills that I had learned in Little League baseball. I left disappointed. I guess I had expected to see these heroes practice hitting a home run in the last of the ninth inning with the score tied or at least practice sliding home on a crucial squeeze bunt. After several hours of reflection, I realized why they were champions. They had been champions in October because they worked on the basics in March. Every so often Christians need to get back to the basics.

Before his public ministry actually began, Jesus acted on his understanding of some of the basics in relating to God. After forty days of wilderness meditation, Jesus was confronted by Satan. Taken to a high mountain and shown the "kingdoms of the world," Jesus heard Satan tempt him with these words: "I will give You all this domain and its glory; . . . Therefore if You worship before me, it shall all be Yours" (Luke 4:6-7). Identifying some of the basics, Jesus responded, "It is written, 'You shall worship the Lord your God and serve Him only' " (Luke 4:8).

One basic way of relating to God is through his Word, the Bible. Jesus made reference to God's Word with the preface to his Old Testament quote of, "It is written." For Jesus, the "written" Word was one of the bases for his authority as well as the basis for his resistance to Satan's temptation. The Bible itself tells us how to relate to God through its use.

Besides taking it to church with you and leaving it on your beside table, what should you be doing with your Bible? Perhaps the first experience you had with the Bible was hearing someone else read from it. You should continue to *hear the Bible* read. Paul said, "Faith comes by hearing, and hearing by the word" (Rom. 10:17). John said, "Blessed is he who reads and those who hear the words" (Rev. 1:3). In addition to hearing the Bible, you ought also to *read the Bible* for yourself. Peter wrote, "Like newborn babes, long for the pure milk of the word" (1 Pet. 2:2), and Paul wrote to Timothy, "Give attention to the public reading of the Scripture" (1 Tim. 4:13).

What are some other ways you ought to be using your Bible? You ought to *study the Bible*. Again Paul wrote Timothy, "Study to shew thyself approved unto God, a workman that needeth not to be ashamed, rightly dividing the word of truth" (2 Tim. 2:15, KJV). It was said of the early Christians, "They received the word with great eagerness, examining the Scriptures daily" (Acts 17:11). And Jesus spoke of searching the Scriptures (see John 5:39).

One of the most overlooked ways of using your Bible to relate to God is meditation. You ought to *meditate on the Bible*. Before day in a quiet place, it could be assumed that Jesus meditated on the Scriptures. Alone and in the dark, he set an example for us (Mark 1:35). Paul instructed Timothy to "Meditate upon these things" (1 Tim. 4:15, KJV). Mary, the mother of Jesus, remembered the word of God through the angel and "pondered [or meditated on] them in her heart" (Luke 2:19, KJV). Continually, the psalmist emphasized meditation (Ps. 1:2; 19:14; 63:6; 119:15, 78,97,148).

There ought to be times in your Christian life when you *memorize the Bible,* especially portions of it that are helpful to you. The psalmist wrote, "Thy word I have treasured in my heart, That I may not sin against Thee" (Ps. 119:11). Both in his temptation experience (Matt. 4:1-11; Deut. 8:3;

6:16; 6:13) and from the cross (Matt. 27:46; Ps. 22:1; Luke 23:46; Ps. 31:5), Jesus quoted from memory portions of Scripture. If you will commit portions of Scripture to memory, Jesus promised the Holy Spirit will "bring to your remembrance all that I said to you" (John 14:26).

The human mind is more amazing than a computer at storing memorized information. I was riding with my host along Makaha Beach in Hawaii when he suddenly pulled off the road at a place where a man was selling shells from the back of his pickup truck. My host exclaimed, "I believe I see a chambered nautilus, and I've been looking for a good one." After I had purchased one of the beautiful shells myself, my host asked what interest I had in a chambered nautilus. At that point I began to quote for him from my own memory the last verse of "The Chambered Nautilus" by Oliver Wendell Holmes:

> Build thee more stately mansions, O my soul,
>   As the swift seasons roll!
>   Leave thy low-vaulted past!
> Let each new temple, nobler than the last,
> Shut thee from heaven with a dome more vast,
>   Till thou at length art free,
> Leaving thine outgrown shell by life's unresting sea![1]

To the amazement of my host, I went on to explain to him that my twelfth-grade English teacher in high school had made us answer the roll by quoting verses of poetry from memory, and that was one verse I had memorized. The point is, it had been over twenty years since I had sat in the classroom at Reagan High School in Houston, Texas, and answered Miss Janie Belle Baten's roll call with that poem, and very few times in those years had I thought about it. Yet, once memorized, that poem had remained in my human computer brain. If the human mind can do such things, how much more can God do with our memorized verses of Scripture?

Finally, you ought to *apply the Bible*. James wrote, "Prove yourselves doers of the word, and not merely hearers" (Jas. 1:22). The writer of Hebrews indicated that those who progress from spiritual "milk" to spiritual "solid food" will do so, "because of practice [or application of the truths related to 'milk']" (Heb. 5:12-14). Jesus used an illustration in teaching his followers that was preceded with a word of application. Before he told of a wise man who built his house upon a rock and a foolish man who built his house upon sand, Jesus likened the wise man to "Whosoever heareth these sayings of mine, and doeth them" (Matt. 7:24, KJV). It is good to hear, read, study, meditate upon, and even memorize God's Word, but it is of extreme importance to apply that Word to your own life and witness. And what will happen if you do these things?

Having heard, read, studied, meditated upon, memorized, and applied the Bible, you will have a better understanding of how to relate to God. You can be absolutely sure when you open your Bible and give it your undivided attention, God will communicate through his Word. But there is another basic that Christians need to get back to.

Worship is a misunderstood and often misplaced basic of the Christian's relationship to God. Satan promised to give Jesus the kingdoms of the world if Jesus would only worship him. Jesus underlined the importance of worship by quoting an Old Testament Scripture, "You shall worship Him [God], and swear by his name" (Deut. 6:13). Other biblical references to worship are found in David's saying, "In the morning, O Lord, Thou wilt hear my voice" (Ps. 5:3). Enoch walked with God (Gen. 5:24). Isaiah's calling was directly related to his worship of God (Isa. 6:1). Jacob worshiped alone (Gen. 28:15-17); and John worshiped on the Isle of Patmos (Rev. 1:10). Both biblical history and personal experience indicate that when the Christian fails to worship consistently, spiritual dryness follows. Worship must go beyond that which is experienced on Sunday.

Did you know that you can worship in ways and at times other than what you experience on Sunday? The Bible speaks of corporate worship, which is what we do on Sunday, but it is more. It is what takes place, or should take place, when two or more are gathered in his name. Corporate worship is beyond the sum total of what you as an individual can offer to God and beyond the sum total of what you as an individual can receive from God. It is group involvement in the company of fellow Christians. The Bible speaks of corporate worship (Gen. 35:2-3; Ex. 24:10-12; Ps.

35:18; Matt. 18:20; Acts 4:31-33; Rom. 15:6; 1 Cor. 14:26; and Heb. 10:25) and encourages our participation in it. The Old Testament is filled with references to family worship as an expression of corporate worship. But there is more to worship of God than what we do in groups, however small or large those groups may be.

When a Christian stands alone before God, the potential of real worship is present. Regardless of the level of commitment, it is still possible for a Christian to fake worship for one hour on Sunday or even around the family altar; but when that Christian stands alone with God, all pretense and ritual disappear. Whereas faking it in a group may be possible, faking it one-to-one is extremely difficult. Arising a great while before day, Jesus placed a high value on private worship as a basic means of relating to God. In addition to the example of Jesus, the Bible speaks of private worship throughout (Gen. 5:24; 28:15-17; Ps. 5:3; Isa. 6:1; Mark 1:35; Rev. 1:10). In light of all this, how important is relating to God through worship?

What do you think is the first business of the church? According to W. T. Conner, former professor of theology at Southwestern Baptist Theological Seminary, "The first business, then, of a church is not evangelism, nor missions, nor benevolence; it is worship. The worship of God in Christ should be at the center of all else the church does. It is the mainspring of all the activity of the church."[2] Whether you agree with Conner or not, worship—adoration, gratitude, repentance, submission, commitment— must be a vital part of your basic relationship to God. There is yet another basic to be considered in relating to God.

"We have met to worship. We depart to serve." That quote or variations of it have appeared in numerous church bulletins. The quote is exactly in keeping with what Jesus had in mind when he responded to Satan's "if you worship me" with the words: "serve Him only." Jesus knew that worship is not complete until it results in service. Thus, one of the basic ways you relate to God is through service to persons. What is service?

Service defined is more than work. It is that for which persons give their entire lives. The broad base of Christian service is seen in 1 Peter 4:10-11, which indicates that anything that is a gift from God can be used in service. The discussion of spiritual gifts in 1 Corinthians 12 supports this fact. One reason God calls people is for service. Israel was selected by God to be a light to the nations. John the Baptist was selected to prepare the way for Jesus. Each disciple was chosen by Jesus with some special service in mind, as well as the overall service of sharing the gospel with the world. But just how important is service?

In comparison to other Christian doctrines, very little is written concerning service. Its importance may be seen in the fact that the same New Testament word translated *worship* is also translated *service*. That explains the various translations of Romans 12:1: "reasonable service" (KJV), "spiritual service of worship" (NASB), "spiritual worship" (NIV). Service and worship are inseparable, and the biblical models are numerous.

Two great models of servanthood stand above the rest in the New Testament. When Jesus described servanthood, he pointed not to the scribe, who was the educated man of the day, nor did he point to the priest, who was the religious man of the day. Jesus pointed to the servant and even claimed identity with the servant. "Who is greater, the one who reclines at table, or the one who serves? Is it not the one who reclines at table? But I am among you as the one who serves" (Luke 22:27). On another occasion Jesus told his disciples, "The greatest among you shall be your servant" (Matt. 23:11). And when the disciples refused to wash one another's feet in the upper room, Jesus looked for a bowl and a towel in order to perform the servant's duty of washing the feet of the disciples (John 13:4-17).

One New Testament personality, more than others, modeled the servant role of Jesus. Even though the world sees him in his greatness, the apostle Paul saw himself as a servant. Paul began Romans by identifying himself as a "bond-servant" (Rom. 1:1). In 1 Corinthians Paul wrote, "For though I am free from all men, I have made myself a slave to all, that I might win the more" (1 Cor. 9:19). In 2 Corinthians Paul wrote, "We do not preach ourselves but Christ Jesus as Lord, and ourselves as your bond-servants for Jesus' sake" (2 Cor. 4:5). Galatians bears these words from Paul, "If I were still trying to please men, I would not be a bond-servant of Christ" (Gal. 1:10). Neglecting to refer to himself in Ephesians as a slave, Paul went a step further and referred to himself as "the prisoner of Christ Jesus" (Eph. 3:1). Beginning his letter to the Philippians, Paul referred to himself, as well as Timothy, as "bond-servants of Christ Jesus" (Phil. 1:1). In Colossians Paul linked himself to servanthood through a reference to "Epaphras, our beloved fellow bond-servant" (Col. 1:7).

Continuing his self-descriptions in the area of servanthood, the apostle Paul described himself as a "fellow-worker in the gospel of Christ" with Timothy in 1 Thessalonians 3:2 and as serving among "perverse and evil men" in 2 Thessalonians 3:2. In 1 Timothy Paul wrote, "I thank Christ Jesus our Lord, who has strengthened me, because He considered me faithful, putting me into service" (1 Tim. 1:12). In 2 Timothy Paul again thanked God "whom I serve with a clear conscience" (2 Tim. 1:3). In his letter to Titus, Paul called himself "a bond-servant" (Titus 1:1), and in his letter to Philemon he called himself a "prisoner of Christ Jesus" and Philemon "a fellow-worker" (Philem. 1). Thus, in all thirteen of Paul's letters, he made reference to his servanthood.

Three basic ways of relating to God have been discussed: relating to God through his Word, the Bible; relating to God through worship of him; and relating to God through our service to persons. So interrelated are these three basics that they support each other and provide a sturdy foundation on which to build a life-style of evangelism. Even a casual look at the Bible shows the importance of worship and service. Worship that does not stem from a biblical base and does not result in service is less than true worship. Service that is not motivated from genuine worship of God and is not modeled after the biblical pattern of servanthood is less than Christian service. These three must go together as basic to the Christian's relationship to God forming the priority of EvangeLife.

Life-style evangelism must begin at the beginning. A friend related to me that when he and his wife married they received a very unusual cookbook as a wedding gift. The first chapter was entitled "Face the Stove." Now that's beginning at the beginning, and that's the idea in EvangeLife. Regardless of how basic or fundamental it may seem, life-style evangelism involves getting back to the basics and developing a meaningful relationship with God. As you go, relate properly to God.

For Further Study

Allen, Roland and Borron, Gordon. *Worship: Rediscovering the Missing Jewell.* Portland: Multnomah Press, 1982.

Chambers, Oswald. *My Utmost for His Highest.* New York: Dodd Mead & Co., 1935.

Conner, W. T. *The Gospel of Redemption.* Nashville: Broadman Press, 1945.

Drummond, Lewis A. *The Revived Life.* Nashville: Broadman Press, 1982.

Foster, Richard J. *Celebration of Discipline.* New York: Harper & Row Publishers, 1978.

Green Michael. *Called to Serve.* Grand Rapids: Baker Book House, 1981.

Hendricks, William. *Doctrine of Man.* Nashville: Convention Press, 1977.

Kung, Hans, translated by Ray and Rosaleen Ockenden. *The Church.* London: Burns & Oates, 1968.

Miller, Keith. *Habitation of Dragons.* Waco: Word Books, 1970.

Packer, J. I. *Evangelism and the Sovereignty of God.* Downers Grove, Il.: Inter Varsity Press, 1961.

Packer, J. I. *Knowing God.* Downers Grove: Inter Varsity Press, 1973.

Segler, Franklin M. *Christian Worship: Its Theology and Practice.* Nashville: Broadman Press, 1967.

Swindoll, Charles R. *Improving Your Serve.* Waco: Word Books, 1981.

Westerhoff, John H. *Inner Growth: Outer Change.* New York: Seabury Press, 1979.

White, Mary. *Successful Family Devotions.* Colorado Springs: Navpress, 1981.

Notes

1. Oliver Wendell Holmes, "The Chambered Nautilus, *"The Complete Poetical Works of Oliver Wendell Holmes* (Boston and New York: Houghton Mifflin Company, 1908), pp.149-150.

2. W. T. Conner, *The Gospel of Redemption* (Nashville: Broadman Press, 1945), p.277.

3

The Model for EvangeLife

The Life-style of Jesus

Role model

Words and people continue to change. In my younger days, I was encouraged to "follow the example" of proper people. Recently I began to hear the term *role model.* Now I am told that much of what you and I learn, we learn from observing role models. My new role models are very similar to my old examples, but I'm trying to change.

As you change, you will be affected by your choice of role models (or examples, if you prefer a former way of life). Your growth as a life-style evangelist will be directed by your evangelistic role model. The options are numerous.

With one word of caution, I suggest the best role model for life-style evangelism is Jesus Christ. He said of himself, "All authority has been given to Me in heaven and on earth" (Matt. 28:18). Since Jesus did not say that of you, model after him with the understanding of the difference that cannot be duplicated.

One other thought related to role model must be shared. There is a difference in a model and a mimic. Webster defines model as "an example for imitation" whereas he defines mimic as "to imitate." To mimic Jesus would be to attempt to live out his life in his style. Life-style evangelism that is modeled after Jesus is his life lived out in your style.

From beginning to earthly end, the style of Jesus was the style of evangelism. The first recorded words of Jesus to his disciples were, "Follow Me, and I will make you fishers of men" (Matt. 4:19). That statement speaks to me of evangelism. The last recorded words of Jesus to his disciples were: "You shall receive power when the Holy Spirit has come

35

upon you; and you shall be My witnesses both in Jerusalem, and in all Judea and Samaria, and even to the remotest part of the earth" (Acts 1:8). Likewise, that statement speaks to me of evangelism. At the beginning and at the end of his earthly ministry, Jesus spoke about evangelism; and in between those two evangelistic poles was a life-style of evangelism.

That which Jesus taught he lived, and that which Jesus lived he taught. For no other teacher would that be totally true. Never did the disciples need to wonder long over some act that Jesus did, for soon he would teach them the "why" of his actions if he had not already done so. Never did the disciples need to wonder long over some teaching of Jesus, for soon he would "flesh out" that teaching in their presence if he had not already done so. The consistency of his life is a style worth modeling.

This chapter presents a case study out of the life and teaching of Jesus. Two passages of Scripture will be considered, two passages that are rather loosely related. Luke 10:25-27 is an incident out of the teaching ministry of Jesus. Mark 6:31-34 is an experience out of the life of Jesus as he related to his disciples. The two, though separated in time and geography, present a united life-style.

Following an exchange related to the law between Jesus and a lawyer, Jesus answered the man's question "Who is my neighbor?" with a parable. Luke recorded it this way:

> A certain man was going down from Jerusalem to Jericho; and he fell among robbers, and they stripped him and beat him, and went off leaving him half dead. And by chance a certain priest was going down on that road, and when he saw him, he passed by on the other side. And likewise a Levite also, when he came to the place and saw him, passed by on the other side. But a certain Samaritan, who was on a journey, came upon him; and when he saw him, he felt compassion, and came to him, and bandaged up his wounds, pouring oil and wine on them; and he put him on his own beast, and brought him to an inn and took care of him. And on the next day he took out two denarii and gave them to the innkeeper and said, "Take care of him; and whatever more you spend, when I return, I will repay you" (Luke 10:30-35).

On another occasion, the size and demand of the crowd was such that Jesus instructed his disciples to join him in an attempt to get away for a while. Mark recorded the story this way:

And they went away in the boat to a lonely place by themselves. And the people saw them going, and many recognized them, and they ran there together on foot from all the cities, and got there ahead of them. And disembarking, He saw a great multitude, and He felt compassion for them because they were like sheep without a shepherd; and He began to teach them many things (Mark 6:32-34).

The Model of Seeing with Sensitivity

In both passages of Scripture, the word *saw* appears. Every character in the two accounts was said to have seen something. In his teaching and in his life, Jesus showed the eye to be a tool for evangelism.

It is possible on certain occasions to see something with the eye and yet never "see" anything. This is exactly what happened to the priest and to the Levite in the first account. Having been trained not to "see," they looked in the ditch and yet did not "see." These religious officials knew that to touch a dead body would render them unclean for seven days (Num. 19:11). Their reasoning might have gone something like this: *if I see someone in need, I might want to get a better look. If I go over to the ditch to get a better look, I might slip and fall into the ditch. If I fall into the ditch, I might touch the person in the ditch. If the person in the ditch is dead, and I touch him, I will be unclean for seven days.* With that kind of logic, it becomes very difficult to "see" human need.

You and I have been guilty of similar logic. In my six years as Baptist Student Union director at the University of Texas, I frequently fell prey to such logic. My logic went something like this: *this is a campus of fifty thousand students. I've got to get from my office to a certain location on campus to meet an appointment. If I take time to look at every student I see, I might see one who needs to talk to me. If I see a student who needs to talk, I will listen. If I listen, I will be late for my appointment. If I am late for my appointment, my reputation of being prompt will be ruined. Thus, I will hurry across the campus and not see anyone.* With logic like that, it is difficult to minister, much less be evangelistic, to some people. So we go on our "priestly" way, unaware of the need around us. That was not the style of Jesus.

The Samaritan "saw" human hurt. Being a part of a half-breed people, the recipient of severe racial hatred, he no doubt "saw" human hurt through his own prejudice. Yet he demonstrated that real, Christlike sight cuts through even something as thick as prejudice.

In the passage from Mark, coming up out of the boat, Jesus "saw" the people. Like sheep without a shepherd, they appeared to Jesus as people with both individual as well as collective hurts. They also appeared to Jesus as people with unlimited potential. Seeing them as beaten travelers in Judean ditches, Jesus also saw them as healed helpers departing wayside inns to walk and talk of their newness.

Aren't you glad that Jesus always saw people not as what they appeared to be but in light of what they could become in him? Check his record. The world saw a cursing, callous fisherman by the name of Simon. Jesus saw one who could preach with such power on the day of Pentecost that thousands would be brought into the kingdom, and he called him Peter. The world saw a tax collector and, in keeping with the common practice, they hated him. Jesus saw one who could later record one of the four Gospel accounts and called him Matthew. The world saw a demoniac and wrote him off as a misfit in society. Jesus saw someone who could witness to an entire city. The world saw a woman living with a man who was not her husband and ridiculed her for that as well as her five previous marriage attempts. Jesus met her at a wellside in Samaria and saw someone who could begin a revival with just her testimony. Aren't you glad Jesus saw more in you than anyone else has ever seen?

I heard Dr. James Pleitz, pastor of the Park Cities Baptist Church in Dallas, Texas, tell about his attempt to purchase a wood carving of a hound dog. After several attempts to praise the wood carver and hopefully lower the price, the old wood-carver replied that it didn't take much effort to carve a hound dog. Said the wood-carver, "You just take a chunk of wood and cut off everything that don't look like a hound dog." The wood-carver could see more in that piece of wood than just wood. Jesus looks at you and me and just "cuts off everything" that doesn't look like him. He sees us in light of what we can become in him, rather than what we are. Aren't you glad?

A life-style of evangelism involves seeing with sensitivity. Both in his teaching and in his life, Jesus modeled this principle for us. But there is a second principle in these passages.

The Model of Feeling Compassion

Religion divorced from feeling is dangerous. Certainly religion with an overemphasis on feeling is dangerous, but religion with *no* feeling is more dangerous. Observe the priest and the Levite. Theirs was a religion without feeling. Not only had they not seen the man in the ditch in a way that would affect them physically but they also felt nothing that would affect them emotionally.

I received a letter from a student summer missionary one summer telling of all the things she had seen in her first days in a large metropolitan area of our country. Surrounding her was a large amount of human need and human hurt. It was obvious that her summer would be full. Years later this summer missionary wrote me that my response to this first letter of hers drastically affected her summer. I had written that I was glad she had seen so much that challenged her. Then I wrote, "When that which you have seen is translated into feeling, you will be ready to be a missionary."

Not only did the Samaritan see human need but he also translated that sight into a feeling of compassion. Compassion is no ordinary feeling but that which comes from the very core of a person's being. In the Gospels the word translated *compassion* is used only to describe the feelings of Jesus with three exceptions. All three exceptions are parables that include Christlike characteristics: the parable of the slave who felt the compassion of his master (Matt. 18:21-35), the parable of the prodigal son who felt the compassion of his father (Luke 15:11-32), and the parable of the good Samaritan who felt compassion for one in need.

One who traveled the road from Jerusalem to Jericho did so with some understanding of danger. The professional thieves who "worked" that road provided for the traveler a rather commonplace scene like the one seen by this Samaritan. Perhaps the Samaritan had himself been a victim of this road. Thus his feeling of compassion may well have been one of identification. Nevertheless, the compassion came from a sensitive seeing of human need. In that sense, the Samaritan was modeling the feelings of Jesus.

Tired, hungry, and in need of retreat, Jesus suggested to his disciples that they go away to a quiet place. God-ordained quiet times are never wasted times, and that time of quiet vacation gave every indication of being just what Jesus and the disciples needed. It would be a good time to relax and review and to return refreshed for even greater ministry, but human need knows no vacation.

Having heard that which touched them at some of their points of need, the crowd raced around the northern shore of the Sea of Galilee faster than the boat carrying the disciples and Jesus could travel. Waiting for them on the northeast shore was the needy crowd. Jesus delayed his vacation to deal with the need of the crowd because he not only saw them but also was "moved with compassion" (Mark 6:34, KJV).

You and I need not only to see people with sensitivity but we need also to feel a Christlike compassion for those whom we see. As we learn to do this, we will discover that seeing and feeling lead to action.

The Model of Action

Faith must have works (Jas. 2:17) and workers. The priest and Levite were unwilling to work out their "faith" in the ditch. Their lack of sight mixed with their lack of feeling produced lack of action. John wrote, "Whoever has the world's goods, and beholds his brother in need and closes his heart ['compassion,' KJV] against him, how does the love of God abide in him?" (1 John 3:17). These two "religious" leaders had refused to help "one of the least of these" (Matt. 25:45) and thus produced a very un-Christlike scene.

A similar scene was witnessed on an interstate highway in Texas. As I drove south toward Austin, I heard a call for help on my C.B. radio. A car was smoking and appeared to be on fire. Someone was calling for a driver with a fire extinguisher. Then I heard a truck driver say, "If it's a four-wheeler on fire, I hope it burns up." About the time I saw the car on the opposite side of the road with people scrambling out of every door, I heard another voice say to the trucker, "Where are you, eighteen-wheeler? I'd like to burn your truck." The trucker replied, "I'm near the Big Mac exit. If you'll burn my truck, I'll collect insurance and get me a new truck." Then he continued, "I wish all the four-wheelers would burn up so we wouldn't have to put up with them on the road." By this time several other truckers had stopped to help with the four-wheeler fire, and I began to lose contact with the angry voices on my C.B. In all fairness to truck drivers, only a very few feel like the one on my C.B. radio that day, but that particular trucker was exhibiting a very un-Christlike spirit. He did not want to see the need. He did not feel anything but contempt for the needy. He did not want to take any action that would be helpful. He did not want to risk his "tough-trucker" image by helping needy four-wheelers.

Action, whatever it's motivation, always involves the possibility of risk. The professional robbers on the Jericho road often placed one of their own in a ditch as a decoy. When some concerned person bent over to offer aid, he was attacked. To work out one's faith feeling in a ditch was to put one's life on the line.

When you and I take action in Christ's name, we can expect risk. Someone will no doubt misunderstand as others misunderstood Jesus. Some well-meaning person will relay our action to another in such a way as to cause a misrepresentation of the truth, a situation not unfamiliar to Jesus. Action will cost you time and talent and energy and perhaps even your reputation. So it was with Jesus.

I have often wondered about the Samaritan in Jesus' parable. Was he on his way home after attending some meeting in Jerusalem? If so, who told his wife and children where he spent the night and why he never made it home that night? Was he on his way to Jericho on business? If so, who told his boss or business associates why he did not show up the morning of the meeting? And don't you know some well-meaning saint had a field day with this bit of gossip: a respectable citizen spent the night taking care of a total stranger in some wayside inn? Who helps hurting Samaritans? Maybe all of this is frightfully close to what Jesus meant by "If anyone wishes to come after Me, let him deny himself, and take up his cross daily, and follow Me" (Luke 9:23).

Coming up out of the boat, seeing the people, and having his heart moved with compassion, Jesus took action. All day long Jesus taught the crowd; and when the day was almost done, he multiplied a boy's lunch and fed the listeners. He put in a good day's work for one who just wanted to get away to a quiet place and "rest awhile." Before that day was fully over, he sent the disciples back to the boat, went up the mountain to pray, called upon the power of God to walk across the water, and caught up with the disciples in the boat. And still he was not through with those shepherd-less "sheep."

The Model of Follow-Through

When you have failed to see with sensitivity, feel compassion, or take action, it becomes very difficult to follow through. A recent experience illustrates this fact. Along with other program personalities for a statewide convention, I was being treated to a preconvention meal in a restaurant. The room was obviously meant to be a private one, yet somehow a young family with two small children had entered the room. Their food order came shortly after ours. One of the members of our party made a very negative statement about another religious group. In the company of Southern Baptist ministers the statement, even though somewhat vicious, was understandable. But in the hearing of the young couple nearby, it was completely out of place and in bad taste. Because I was sitting where I could see the couple, I noticed some uneasiness at their table and tried to call this to the attention of my fellow minister but without success.

As if enough damage had not already been done, my friend continued to criticize his religious target. Finally, he quit, but I sensed that the damage had been done. As we left the restaurant, the young wife at the adjoining table asked, "Excuse me, but could I ask what church you are with?"

My talkative friend replied, with too much pride for the moment, "We're Southern Baptists, how about you folks?"

I was hoping that she would be more caring than he because I had a nagging feeling related to her answer. Sure enough, her answer revealed their church to be the same one my friend had been criticizing. I felt helpless. We had not seen with sensitivity, nor had we felt any compassion even for the uneasiness in the room, and our actions had certainly left much to be desired. How do you follow through on that? Hindsight is alway best, and I have thought of several positive things I could have done. But on that day, I simply smiled at the couple and left the room for my friend to answer for himself.

The evidence of the priest and Levite indicates that it is very difficult to follow through on nothing. They could not follow through on what they had seen, for they had seen nothing. They could not follow through on what they had felt, for they had felt nothing. They could not follow through on their action, for they had taken no action. Follow-through gives authenticity to witness, and the lack of it is an indictment against failure.

The Samaritan modeled followed through in a beautiful way. After spending the night taking care of the one who had been left for dead in the ditch, he then said to the innkeeper, "Whatever more you spend, when I return, I will repay you" (Luke 10:35). To meet human need partially when one has the resources to meet it completely is inconsistent with the concept of total commitment to Jesus Christ.

The experience in the life of Jesus shared by Mark is picked up in John for the events of the next day. When Jesus and his disciples arrived in Capernaum, the crowd was again waiting on them. This time Jesus taught the cost of discipleship, and the crowd's response was different: "This is a difficult statement; who can listen to it?" (John 6:60). Having said this, the crowd left Jesus alone with his disciples. He had followed through to tell the crowd why they should follow him. Even though this crowd left, not all who heard the why of following Jesus left. Seeing, feeling, and acting by themselves are not enough. Without the why of it all, false witness has been borne. There comes a time when the name above every name must be named.

Life-style evangelism was modeled by Jesus both in his teaching and in his personal ministry. Other case studies from his life will reveal still other characteristics for you and I to model. As you go, model Jesus.

For Further Study

Armastorg, Richard Stoll. *Service Evangelism*. Philadelphia: Westminster Press, 1979.
Barclay, William. *The Mind of Jesus*. New York: Harper & Row Publishers, 1960.
Bruce, A. B. *The Training of the Twelve*. Grand Rapids: Kregel Press, 1971.
Griffith, Leonard. *Encounters With Christ*. New York: Harper & Row Publishers, 1965.

Hendrix, John and Householder, Lloyd. *The Equipping of Disciples.* Nashville: Broadman Press, 1977.

Hunter, Archibald M. *The Work and Words of Jesus.* Philadelphia: Westminster Press, 1950, 1973.

Miles, Delos. *How Jesus Won Persons.* Nashville: Broadman Press, 1982.

Miles, Delos. *Master Principles of Evangelism.* Nashville: Broadman Press, 1982.

Rinker, Rosalind. *Who Is This Man?* Grand Rapids: Zondervan Publishing House, 1960.

Stalker, James. *The Life of Jesus Christ.* Westwood, N.J.: Fleming H. Revell Co., 1891.

Stewart, James S. *The Life and Teachings of Jesus Christ.* New York: Abingdon Press, n.d.

Thomson, James G. S. S. *The Praying Christ.* Grand Rapids: Wm. B. Eerdmans Publishing Co., 1959.

Trueblood, Elton. *Confronting Christ.* Waco: Word Books, 1960.

Wilson, Carl. *With Christ in the School of Disciple Building.* Grand Rapids: Zondervan Publishing House, 1976.

4

The Power for EvangeLife

The Holy Spirit in You

The United States has a population of 235 million. Of this number, an estimated 82 million are over the work age leaving 153 million people to do the work. Subtract the approximately 85 million persons who are below the work age, and you have 68 million people to do the majority of the work. There are also an estimated 34,471,002 persons employed by the federal government in some capacity which leaves only 33,528,998 to do the remainder of the work. The 10 million or so in the armed forces leave only 23,528,998 to do the rest of the work, and when you subtract from this number the 20 million or so who are in hospitals or similar places, the national work force is reduced to 1,528,998. There are an estimated 1,128,500 bums, vagrants, or others with a pathological fear of work. That leaves only 400,498 to carry the remainder of the national work load, 400,496 of whom are presently behind bars. Which, my friend, leaves you and me, and explains why we are so tired and in need of extra energy.

Whereas, the above figures may not be totally accurate, we do sometimes feel overworked and even get weary in well doing. Among other things, the Holy Spirit was given to believers as an energy source, an extra power for life-style evangelism. Never were we meant to live the Christian life in our own strength. Power is available.

The Power of the Holy Spirit in Perspective

When the believer is filled with the Holy Spirit, several aspects of life are no longer under human power. The apostle Paul wrote, "Do not get drunk with wine . . . but be filled with the Spirit" (Eph. 5:18). At a recent baseball game, I sat behind a man who drank at least one beer per inning and in long innings, he consumed more than one. Watching him get drunk on beer helped me to understand the parallel that Paul was trying to make.

Holy Spirit power cleanses the believer. From his conversation, I learned that this man had undergone a frustrating day at the office. It was obvious that he was trying to cleanse his day through the consumption of beer. Washing away troubles may be temporarily possible via alcoholic beverage, but there is a better way. Who, of all persons, should have their troubles washed away more consistently than the believer who is cleansed by the power of the Holy Spirit? Having experienced cleansing, one is ready for control.

Holy Spirit power controls the believer. I'm not sure how many drinks he had consumed before arriving at the baseball game, but by the third inning, I noticed that he was losing control. For one thing, his speech was affected. His speech became more invincible, more constant, and to some degree more bold. Whereas, in the first inning he did not like the umpire, by the third inning he wanted to kill the umpire. At the beginning of the game, he knew nobody around him. By the fourth inning, my semi-intoxicated friend was talking to everyone around him, even those of us who did not care to listen.

Who of all persons should be more under control by an outside force which has been internalized than the believer under control of Holy Spirit power? For one thing, that Holy Spirit power should control our speech, making us more invincible, more constant, and even more bold. Cleansed and controlled, the believer is also carried.

Holy Spirit power carries the believer. By the sixth inning beer that the man was consuming was carrying him obviously to certain other parts of the stadium. But of greater interest to me was the fact that the alcohol's influence was slowly transforming my friend into an expert on baseball. Instructions to the coaches, advice to the players, and even assistance to vendors and ushers in the stands were all a part of his seventh inning stretch which lasted two outs into the inning. Mentally and emotionally, this person was being carried to territory that he would not have otherwise gone. Who of all persons ought to be carried not only to geographical but also to spiritual realms to which they could not go on their own power than believers who are under internalized outside power? Submitting to another power carries us beyond our own abilities.

Recently, I found myself with a tight schedule. I was to speak at Ridgecrest, North Carolina, on Saturday morning and at Glorieta, New Mexico, the next day, Sunday morning. There was no way, in my own power, that I could make both responsibilities. But after completing my assignment in Ridgecrest, I boarded a jet, sat back and relaxed, submitting to another power source, and in just a few hours, was in Glorieta in time to get a short night's sleep before my Sunday speaking responsibility. Jet power is greater than human power, but it is also more dangerous, involving more risk. Some people never submit to it and, thus, never are able to be carried by it to places that they could not get on their own power. I have learned when I run the risk of submitting to a power greater than my own—that of the Holy Spirit—I am able to cover more territory, both physical and spiritual. The Holy Spirit's power cleanses, controls, carries, and also completes.

Holy Spirit power completes the believer. When the game was over, an usher had to help the now-intoxicated man up the stairs to a telephone. I concluded that the process of submitting to an intoxicating power was complete. At a speaking engagement within the past month, I used this illustration and confessed that I was not sure exactly how to draw my fourth analogy of completeness. One of the men in the group to whom I was speaking said, "Take it from a member of Alcoholics Anonymous, beer will make you complete—at least for a short time." Who of all persons should be more completed by another power source than the believer who has submitted to the Holy Spirit? We are completed at points like our prayer life. When, in our own weakness, we do not remember how to pray as we ought, "the Spirit also helps our weakness; for we do not know how to pray as we should, but the Spirit Himself intercedes for us" (Rom. 8:26).

Having submitted to the Holy Spirit's power and having been cleansed, controlled, carried, and completed by it, one wonders why we do not remain in that condition. However, sin takes its toll on our lives, and we do not remain empowered by God's Spirit. To be intoxicated with the Holy Spirit, as Paul instructed, is to know power in EvangeLife. We need to pray with the psalmist, "Create in me a clean heart, O God, And *renew* a steadfast spirit within me" (Ps. 51:10, Author's italics). Oh, for the renewing energy of the Holy Spirit!

The Power of the Holy Spirit in a Word: *Energy*

Nine times in the New Testament the Greek word *energeia* is used, each time by the apostle Paul. Never used to describe human power, this word, from which we obviously get our English word *energy,* is always used to describe divine power in action. In these nine uses, we can see the potential of God's power, the use of God's power, and the misuse of God's power. *Energeia* is variously translated power, might, work.

How much power does God have? Of the nine uses of *energeia,* five are related to the potential of God's power. In Ephesians 1:19-20, Paul asked this very question concerning the potential of God's power, then gave one answer: "What is the surpassing greatness of His power toward us who believe. These are in accordance with the working of the strength of His might which He brought about in Christ, when He raised Him from the dead, and seated Him at His right hand in the heavenly places" (Eph. 1:19-20). Using the word *energeia* twice in this reference, Paul stated that God's power could raise Jesus from the dead. In another letter, Paul made a similar reference: "Having been buried with him in baptism and raised with him through your faith in the power of God, who raised him from the dead" (Col. 2:12, NIV). In addition to God's power being used to raise Jesus from the dead, there are other examples of the potential of God's power.

How much power does God have? In writing to the church in Ephesus, Paul stated, "From whom the whole body fitly joined together and compacted by that which every joint supplieth, according to the effectual working in the measure of every part, maketh increase of the body unto the edifying of itself in love" (Eph. 4:16, KJV). Paul was teaching that the power of God is what held the body—the church—together. A fifth use of the word *energeia* indicates the power of God is that which changes the human body at the end of this life. "For our citizenship is in heaven, from which also we eagerly wait for a Savior, the Lord Jesus Christ; who will transform the body of our humble state into conformity with the body of

His glory, by the exertion of the power that He has even to subject all things to Himself" (Phil. 3:20-21). Now we need to look at the ways God allows his power to be used.

How can we use God's power? The very same word, *energeia,* which described the potential of God's power was also used twice to describe how Paul used power in his ministry. Paul wrote, "I became a servant of this gospel by the gift of God's grace given me through the working of his power" (Eph. 3:7, NIV). It was through God's power that Paul found his strength for service. He also wrote, "To this end I labor, struggling with all his energy, which so powerfully works in me" (Col. 1:29, NIV). Paul found strength for his work in the power of God. As we serve God and work the work that he has given us to do, we have at our availability *energeia*—the kind of power that God used to raise Jesus from the dead, to hold the church together, and to change earthly bodies into heavenly bodies. The implementing of that kind of power is certain to arouse Satan's curiosity.

How does Satan attempt to use God's power? If you don't know by now, you will soon learn that anytime God has something good working, Satan always tries to get in on it. So it is with *energeia.* Twice in the Scriptures, the word *energeia* is used to describe the activity of Satan. Paul wrote: "The Wicked One will come with the power of Satan and perform all kinds of false miracles and wonders, and use every kind of wicked deceit on those who will perish. They will perish because they did not welcome and love the truth so as to be saved. And so God sends the power of error to work in them so that they believe what is false" (2 Thess. 2:9-11, GNB). Even though Satan is allowed to misuse the power of *energeia,* it is obvious that it is God who supplies the power and allows the misuse of it. In so doing, God continues to control *energeia.* With God as the source of power, it is available to be used.

Where do we get God's power? With the nine uses of *energeia* having already been cited and reference made to God being the source of power, we will have to turn to other Greek words for *power* to discover how to appropriate God's power. One source of God's power is his Word, the Bible. The writer of Hebrews wrote, "For the word of God is quick, and powerful, and sharper than any two-edged sword" (Heb. 4:12, KJV). Paul wrote, "And we also thank God continually because, when you received the word of God, which you heard from us, you accepted it not as the word of men, but as it actually is, the word of God, which is at work in you who believe" (1 Thess. 2:13, NIV). This powerful word of God is already at work in the believer providing for us God's power. A second source of God's power is through prayer. James wrote, "The prayer of a righteous man is powerful and effective" (Jas. 5:16, NIV). Prayer may be seen as the key that releases God's power. With these facts concerning *energeia,* there is little reason for the believer to ever be powerless.

The Power of the Holy Spirit in Your Testimony

"I know I ought to witness, but I just can't." That is an all too familiar response of Christians when confronted with the biblical teachings on witnessing. My response to one who posed that excuse to me in a recent seminar was, "You're right! *You* can't witness, nor was it ever intended that *you* do so. The Bible clearly teaches that witnessing is plural, not singular." The pressure of being a singular witness is relieved when one reads, "We are witnesses to these things—we and the Holy Spirit, who is God's gift to those who obey him" (Acts 5:32, GNB). Jesus told his disciples, "He [Holy Spirit] will bear witness of Me, and you will bear witness also" (John 15:26-27). God's power—*energeia*—is available to you as you share your testimony. Relax, success is not dependent upon you; take a deep breath, and share your testimony in the power of the Holy Spirit, and leave the results in the hands of a powerful God. As you prepare to share your testimony, several suggestions may prove helpful.

Your testimony is unique. Among other reasons, your testimony has within it the added dimension of the Holy Spirit's power. If I share with you my personal testimony of a recent trip to Europe, it would have no power in it other than the power that I might generate. I might be so persuasive in my presentation of the details of that trip that you would decide to go to Europe and even fly on Air France Airlines, but no outside power would participate in the telling of that testimony. Now, if I share with you what God has done and is doing in my life, a unique sense of power does two things as I share. For one, the Holy Spirit indwells and empowers the testimony as I voice it; and, second, the Holy Spirit convicts you as you hear it. My personal testimony—and yours—is unique.

Your testimony is authoritative. In the United States, it takes only one reputable eyewitness to prove a case in our courts. In a country that places that much authority on one eyewitness testimony—allowing a person to be imprisoned or even executed on one testimony—your personal testimony has authority. Share your testimony with God-empowered authority.

Your testimony is relevant. That which you share of your relationship with God will be rooted in the past as you tell of life before Christ and relay your conversion experience and early Christian growth. However, your testimony must not emphasize the past to the extent that it de-emphasizes the present. If, in sharing with you the personal testimony of my marriage, I told you that I was married to Joanne Cunningham of San Antonio, Texas, on August 8, 1964, at 3:00 PM in the Trinity Baptist Church of San Antonio, and in the year 2014 we plan to celebrate our fiftieth anniversary, what do you know of my marriage that is helpful? You know about as much as I would know of your Christian testimony if you told me that you became a Christian at age ten and you plan on going to heaven when you die. A relevant testimony is up-to-date, meaningful, as my marriage testimony would be if I shared with you how God is working in our family now. Update your testimony as God continues to work powerfully in your life.

Your testimony should avoid excessive details and negative statements. Whereas the details make it personal, rather than a xeroxed copy of someone else's testimony, excess details tend to become boring to an uninformed listener. Unless it was Billy Graham or some other well-known person, the name of the person preaching in the service where you made a public profession of your faith is excess since the listener would not know the preacher. Too many references to self, especially preconversion references to self, make the testimony negative. Share what life was like before Christ but not to the extent that you glorify the non-Christian life-style and present a negative Christian testimony. I grew up in a day when some youth evangelists so glorified their lives of sin before they met Christ and spent so little time on their positive Christian experiences that some of my peers decided to go out and "get a testimony." The effect was negative because the emphasis was on self rather than on Jesus Christ. Share a positive, persuasive testimony.

Your testimony should be in the language of the people. Christians are loaded with inchurch terminology. We understand what we mean when talking to each other; but the non-Christians, especially if they have not been raised in a church, do not understand our language. Did you ever sit in a doctor's office and listen to him share with you the results of his examination and not know what he was talking about because he used medical terminology? That is the way the non-Christians feel when, looking at them as "prospects," we "share" with them the "grace" of God, urging them to get under "conviction" and "invite Jesus into their hearts," so that they can "get saved" out of "the world in which they live," get "washed in the blood of the Lamb," and join the "fellowship of the saints." I understand every part of that statement, and perhaps you do also; but do the non-Christians with whom we are trying to communicate the good news of Jesus Christ understand? Share your testimony in terminology they can understand.

Your testimony is important enough to prepare. A call to share is a call to prepare, so let me suggest that you write out your testimony. Perhaps you could allow a Christian friend to read it or listen as you read it for the purpose of constructive criticism. Read your testimony in light of the preceding suggestions. Rewrite it again until you have a testimony that communicates. Preparation will also allow you to cover the important facts as you condense your testimony. It is far easier for most people to elaborate than to condense. If you will prepare a condensed version of your testimony, you can elaborate as time and interest allow. On the other hand, if you have a long testimony, you may not be able to share it in a brief encounter. I have jokingly said that I have two testimonies—an elevator testimony and a coast-to-coast-flight testimony. What I really mean is that I have a condensed version that can be given in less than two minutes and a long version that can be given at whatever length the listener is interested in hearing. Prepare your testimony, and share it in the power of the Holy Spirit.

Your testimony is a part of a larger plan. Since "we are witnesses to these things—we and the Holy Spirit"—let's define the responsibilities.

God has assigned to the Holy Spirit numerous tasks, some of which we would rather do ourselves. Most Christians enjoy that part of witnessing that convicts the non-Christian. We can really elaborate on "all have sinned" (Rom. 3:23) and even get specific. Likewise, most Christians enjoy that part of witnessing that converts the non-Christian to Christ. We can really emphasize "Behold, I stand at the door and knock" (Rev. 3:20) to the point we almost open the door for them. Both of these tasks—conviction and conversion—have been assigned to the Holy Spirit (John 16:7-15). Your testimony fits into this larger plan as you share what God has done in your life—your testimony—and what you know from your reading of the Bible he can do in another's life—the plan of salvation. Allow the Holy Spirit to do his work, understand that others will also be a part of the witnessing process, share faithfully your testimony and the plan of salvation, and let God's power generate the results. With this in mind and in practice, it is impossible to fail. It is likewise foolish to claim, "I led him (or her) to Christ." You might more correctly say, "I was a part of a greater plan that resulted in him (or her) becoming a Christian." Understand your role in a larger plan. Having looked at the power of the Holy Spirit in perspective, in a word—*energeia,* and in your testimony, you should be better prepared to put into practice plural witnessing in God's power.

A family gave what they thought to be a relatively worthless piece of land to a Christian institution as a part of their will. When all members of the family had died and the will was probated, the property was turned over to the Christian institution. Several years later, after numerous attempts to sell the property, an individual on the adjacent piece of property drilled for and struck oil. Suddenly, the property owned by the Christian institution became extremely valuable. They now possessed wealth and power, whereas they thought they possessed only land. The most interesting commentary on the story related to earlier years when the original family owners had survived the Great Depression, but only with great difficulty. One person exclaimed, "They were powerless, when just below the surface was all the power they could possibly have wanted." Many times we live our Christian lives and participate in Christian witness as if we were powerless, when just below the surface—just on the inside of us—there lives the greatest source of power we could ever desire. Power is useless until you tap the source of it. You have God's *energeia,* his Holy Spirit power, available to you. As you go, go in God's power.

For Further Study

Augsburger, David W. *Communicating Good News.* Scottsdale, Pa. and Newton, Ka.: Mennonite Publishing House and Faith & Life Press, 1972.

Conner, W. T. *The Work of the Holy Spirit.* Nashville: Broadman Press, 1940.

Graham, Billy. *The Holy Spirit: Activating God's Power in Your Life.* Waco: Word Books, 1978.

Green, Michael. *I Believe in the Holy Spirit.* Grand Rapids: Wm. B. Eerdmans Publishing Co., 1975.

Griffith-Thomas, W. H. *The Holy Spirit of God.* Grand Rapids: Wm. B. Eerdmans Publishing Co., 1955.

Harkness, Georgia. *The Fellowship of the Holy Spirit.* Nashville: Abingdon Press, 1966.

Leavell, Landrum P. *God's Spirit in You.* Nashville: Broadman Press, 1974.

Leavell, Landrum P. *The Doctrine of the Holy Spirit.* Nashville: Convention Press, 1983.

Neighbour, Ralph, Jr. *The Touch of the Spirit.* Nashville: Broadman Press, 1972.

Ogilvie, Lloyd John. *Drumbeat of Love.* Waco: Word Books, 1976.

Stagg, Frank. *The Holy Spirit Today.* Nashville: Broadman Press, 1973.

Starkey, Lycurgus M. *The Holy Spirit at Work in the Church.* Nashville and New York: Abingdon Press, 1965.

Stott, John R. W. *Baptism and Fullness: The Work of the Holy Spirit Today.* Downers Grove: Inter Varsity Press, 1976.

Young, J. Terry. *The Spirit Within You.* Nashville: Broadman Press, 1977.

5

The Application of EvangeLife

Relationship to the World

A tire manufacturer used to advertise that the tires they sold were better "where the rubber meets the road." That is like my grandfather's saying about where the "water meets the wheel." The real test of a product or of an idea is when it meets the test of application. A tire is of little use if it cannot meet the road and do it's job. Water generates power when it meets the wheel. The acid test of life-style evangelism comes when it meets the non-Christian world. It will either change that world or be changed by the world's influence.

J. B. Phillips translates Romans 12:2 in a way that illustrates the point: "Don't let the world around you squeeze you into its own mould, but let God remake you so that your whole attitude of mind is changed. Thus you will prove in practice that the will of God's good, acceptable to him and perfect" (Rom. 12:2, Phillips). How are we to live in relationship to this non-Christian world?

Application Through Relationship to the World

Let's begin with a definition of the world and an identification of its leader. The apostle Paul described the world as "dark" when he wrote, "For our struggle is not against flesh and blood, but against rulers, against the authorities, against the powers of this dark world and against the spiritual forces of evil in the heavenly realms" (Eph. 6:12, NIV). Earlier in that same Ephesian letter, Paul had identified Satan as "the ruler of the kingdom of the air" (Eph. 2:2, NIV). But what did Jesus have to say about this world and its leader?

Jesus knew the evils of this world and told his disciples, "Behold, I send you out as sheep in the midst of wolves" (Matt. 10:16). He likewise knew who was responsible for the evil in this world and pointed to Satan as "the ruler of this world" (John 12:31). On the surface, the prospect of living as "sheep" in a world of "wolves," especially where it is "dark," is not too exciting. But there is a way to relate to that kind of world.

Our relationship to the world was described by Paul in Romans 12:2. Whereas, J. B. Phillips translated the verse using the words *mould* and *remake,* the *New American Standard Bible* says, "Do not be conformed to this world, but be transformed by the renewing of your mind" (Rom. 12:2). The concept is found in these two words—*mould/re-make* or *conformed/transformed.* The Greek words are *schēma* and *morphē. Schēma* refers to the outward, changable aspect of something, whereas *morphē* refers to the inward, unchanging part. Let me illustrate.

In relation to *morphē,* from which we get our word *metamorphosis* —change by a supernatural means, I would refer to myself as a male. I had no personal choice in that matter, and I cannot of myself change my maleness. Part of my *morphē* is maleness. In relation to *schēma*—from which we get our word *scheme* to form a plan as in the scheme of things—I would refer to myself as once being a male baby in diapers, a boy-male playing Little League baseball, a teenage male, a college male, a single adult male, a married male, a father male, and now a middle-age crisis male. The maleness (*morphē*) did not change, but the outward form (*schēma*) according to the plan of God changed as I grew older. Now let's look again at what Paul said about relating to the world.

Paul said we are not to be conformed (*schēma*) to the world, but we are to be transformed (*morphē*). That is, our priority in relating to the world is not to look like, walk like, talk like, or smell like the world but rather to be different on the inside where a miracle has taken place. God has changed that part of us that we cannot change. We are transformed in him, no longer conformed to the world. We are still in this world; but as believers in Jesus Christ, we are no longer of this world.

A word of caution is in order before proceeding further. This is the same apostle Paul who, on another occasion, wrote, "I have become all things to all men, that I may by all means save some" (1 Cor. 9:22). Paul did not want Christians conforming to the world; yet, at the same time, he did not want Christians to so withdraw from the world that they lost their ability to communicate with and witness to the world. Withdrawal to the point of becoming weird is not transformation. Remember, we are still in this world, but in Christ we are no longer of this world.

Jesus had much to say about the believer's relationship to the non-Christian world. Jesus said of himself, "I am not of this world" (John 8:23), and of his disciples, "You are not of the world" (John 15:19); yet being in this world, he described his disciples as "salt" (Matt. 5:13) and "light" (Matt. 5:14) and the kingdom of heaven as "leaven" (Matt. 13:33). I seriously doubt if you have ever come away from a meal exclaiming, "That sure was good salt!" You may have made mention that there was too much or not enough salt in the food; but when salt is doing its work, you are unaware of it. Salt "glorifies" that which it relates too if the relationship is in order. Likewise, light and leaven call no attention to themselves unless they are out of proportion but "glorify" that to which they relate. When the transformed Christian relates properly to the world, Jesus Christ is glorified, not the Christian. We are to lift him up, not ourselves. We work, as it were, behind the scenes while he gets the spotlight. Beware of any Christian who demands the spotlight. We are to be light, not in the light.

One more thing related to our Lord's description of his disciples: food does not affect salt, rather salt affects food. Darkness does not affect light, rather light affects darkness. The lump does not affect the leaven, rather the leaven affects the lump. Follow the logic a step further. The world does not affect the Christian, rather the Christian affects the world. Who are you when you're not around Christians? When you are the only Christian in a group, do you desire to become like the group; or do those around you, even though they might never admit it, desire to become like you? For them to desire becoming like you should be a step in their desire to become like Christ, if you are living a Christlike life. Be like salt and leaven and affect your world. But remember your armor.

Application to the World—Equipped with God's Armor

I heard about a boxer who, in the process of getting beat up, kept coming to his corner at the end of each round only to hear his manager say, "He's never touched you yet champ." After several rounds of this and with his nose bleeding and eyes swollen shut, the boxer exclaimed to his manager, "Well, would you keep an eye on the referee for me. Somebody out there is beating the daylights out of me." You may not know who it is but, if you're trying to live a Christlike life in the midst of a non-Christian world, somebody is beating the daylights out of you. Let me tell you who it is: it's none other than Satan himself. He doesn't like it when you live a Christlike life, and he gets especially furious when you begin to evangelize the non-Christian.

It was to just this kind of situation that Paul wrote:

> Be strong in the Lord, and in the strength of His might. Put on the full armor of God, that you might be able to stand firm against the schemes of the devil. For our struggle is not against flesh and blood, but against the rulers, against the powers, against the world forces of this darkness, against the spiritual forces of wickedness in the heavenly places. Therefore, take up the full armor of God, that you may be able to resist in the evil day, and having done everything, to stand firm" (Eph. 6:10-13).

You were never meant to relate to this non-Christian world unequipped. God has provided his own armor for you. Let's look at that armor.

Most of the armor of God is defensive equipment. That does not mean that we are to spend the majority of our time defending the faith. It simply implies that our one offensive weapon—the Word of God—is adequate for the encounter. But first, a look at the defensive armor.

"Stand firm therefore, having girded your loins with truth" (Eph. 6:14). The first piece of armor mentioned by Paul is truth. On the surface, it would seem that armor would weigh one down in the battle. Paul began with truth, for it is that which sets us free (John 8:32). Our business as evangelists is to set persons free from the bondage of sin. Truth will do just that, but it will also protect us. I would rather stand with a minority on the grounds of truth than stand with an overwhelming majority on the grounds of falsehood. Truth will win; in Christ, it has already won, regardless of the odds against it. Jesus Christ, the same yesterday, today, and forever, is truth; and in that fact, we find security and safety. But not everyone agrees with that fact.

The prayer was not eloquent, but I had made reference to a quote that bothered the speaker of the evening. It was the graduation ceremony at the University of Texas, and it was the Baptist's year to pray. As the Baptist campus minister, I was just doing my duty in relation to the university. As we marched in dressed in our academic colors, looking for all the world like a funeral procession for peacocks, I was attracted again to the words inscribed in marble over the doors to the main building. We would sit during the ceremony, just under that inscription and face the students and guests seated on the lawn. The quote was from the Bible, "Ye shall know the truth, and the truth shall make you free" (John 8:32, KJV). I found it fitting to call attention to that quote in my invocation. I had a feeling very few eyes were closed anyway. Then I thanked God for sending Jesus Christ—the truth—to set us free. The commencement speaker was president of a southwest university noted for its academic standing and was, no doubt, an extremely well-educated man himself. I could tell that by his colors. In his speech, just as most of the audience was falling asleep, this president turned to where I sat on the platform and said, "I must correct the Reverend Mr. Crawford's prayer of a few moments ago. Truth is relative! It is not embodied in any one person." Well, I sat there and smiled. I knew two things: the Bible had told me he was mistaken, and I had the benediction in which to make a rebuttal. Truth is not relative. It finds its best expression in the Person of Jesus Christ and suits us well as our first piece of armor. But there is more.

"Stand firm therefore, . . . having put on the breastplate of righteousness" (Eph. 6:14). As if truth were not enough security, the psalmist said, "I have been young, and now I am old;/Yet I have not seen the righteous forsaken" (Ps. 37:25). Paul wrote to Timothy concerning a "crown of righteousness" (2 Tim. 4:8), and we sometimes sing, "dressed in his righteousness alone, Faultless to stand before the throne." Equipped with righteousness we not only feel secure but we know that even in the end we will be found "faultless" and rewarded with a victor's crown. That's good news to the battle weary. But there is more.

"And having shod your feet with the preparation of the gospel of peace" (Eph. 6:15). Putting on peace allows one to relax in the midst of conflict because it is a different kind of peace than that which the world gives. Jesus said to his disciples, "Peace I leave with you; My peace I give you; not as the world gives, do I give to you" (John 14:27). God's peace, given to us by Jesus Christ, is peace with God, with others, and with self; and the world cannot comprehend it. It is indeed a peace "which surpasses all comprehension"; and as defensive armor, it shall "guard your hearts and your minds in Christ Jesus" (Phil. 4:7). Yet there is more armor.

"In addition to all, taking up the shield of faith with which you will be able to extinguish all the flaming missiles of the evil one" (Eph. 6:16). The application and use of a shield is obvious, but a shield of faith will always look foolish to nonbelievers. Abraham looked foolish to nonbelievers. He was asked why he was packing for a journey and where he was going. His response was that he did not know. Now that looks foolish. You would not pack and prepare for a journey without knowing your destination, but that is exactly what Abraham did, and it looked foolish. God had told Abraham, "Leave your native land, your relatives, and your father's home, and go to a country that I am going to show you" (Gen. 12:1, GNB). Abraham, as well as others, looked foolish when they employed faith.

There is a fine line between faith and foolishness. What the believer sees as faith, the nonbeliever sees as foolishness. Sometimes the truth is known only in retrospect. Noah looked foolish building an ark, miles from water. When asked where the water was coming from to float his boat, Noah probably told them what God had said, that it was going to rain. Since rain falling from the sky had not been previously mentioned in history, Noah's friends must have had a good laugh at that prediction. But they quit laughing when it began to sprinkle, "And the rain fell upon the earth for forty days and forty nights" (Gen. 7:12). Noah and his family survived through faith while the nonbelievers perished through foolishness.

The apostle Paul was thought to be foolish when in reality he was being faithful. Here was a man who had already attained greatness. He was already the leader of the Jewish persecution of Christians. Had Paul never become a Christian, the probability is that he would still have been mentioned in history. Yet he gave up greatness, and all its benefits, for the life-style of a first-century Christian. Someone must have called him a fool, for Paul responded, "We are fools for Christ's sake" (1 Cor. 4:10). When you put on faith, you not only protect yourself but also look foolish to nonbelievers. There is still one more piece of defensive armor.

"Take the helmet of salvation" (Eph. 6:17). The wording is signficantly different for this piece of armor. All other pieces we are to put on or pick up, but the helmet of salvation we are to "take" or receive as one would receive a gift. Indeed, salvation is a gift from God (Eph. 2:8). So important is this helmet of salvation that even the Lord wears it. According to Isaiah, "He put . . . the helmet of salvation on his head" (Isa. 59:17, NIV). Equipped with this defensive armor, we are now ready to look at the one offensive weapon.

"And take . . . the sword of the Spirit, which is the word of God" (Eph. 6:17). The purpose of this sword is not to defend ourselves but rather to redeem the world. Reduced to a simple definition, the purpose of the Bible is the redemption of sinful humanity through the revelation of God. *Redemption* is not a difficult word to understand. My wife used to collect savings stamps. There was a time when we were fanatics about savings stamps. We bought groceries only on Wednesday because that was double stamp day, and we bought gasoline only on Monday because that was double stamp day. We had a catalog of gifts that could be ours in return for the stamps. When we decided on a particular gift and collected the right number of stamp books, we would take the stamps to a store that had a sign on it reading "Redemption Center." Inside the store, we would "redeem" our stamps. The process of trading in one item of value, the stamps, for an item of greater value was called "redemption." The process is similar related to spiritual matters. One day I traded in my life for a life of greater value from God. We call it "new life" or "new birth," but it is in essence a replacement of the old life for the new. The process is called "redemption," and that is the purpose of the Bible, our sword.

This redemptive purpose runs throughout the Bible. In Genesis 1—2, redemption was designed or planned. Before God ever said, "Let there be . . ." he had a plan for the world, and that plan included redemption. In Genesis 3:1 to 11:26, redemption became required. Humanity sinned and thereby required a redemptive process to reunite the broken fellowship with God. In Genesis 11:27 to Malachi 4:6, redemption was prepared for. Through a people, then a nation, then a family, then the line of David, redemption was narrowed down to the focal point of all history: the birth of the Redeemer. In the Gospels—Matthew, Mark, Luke, and John—we have redemption effected. It was effected in the person of Jesus Christ. In the Book of Acts we have redemption shared. It was shared first with Jerusalem, then Judea and Samaria, and ultimately with the ends of the earth. In The New Testament letters, those of Paul as well as the general letters, we have redemption explained. Paul became the great explainer of redemption, joined by James, Peter, John, Jude, and the writer of Hebrews. In the Book of Revelation, we have redemption realized. Ultimately that which we know only in part will be known fully and that which "we see through a glass, darkly" we shall see face-to-face (1 Cor. 13:12, KJV). Redemption will be realized. So from beginning to end, our sword —the Bible—has as its purpose the redemption of humanity.[1] But even though Paul had listed the armor of God, he was not yet through with the subject of equipping.

A part of the armor or God's extra resource was noted by Paul in the equipping prayer: "With all prayer and petition pray at all times in the Spirit, and with this in view, be on the alert with all perseverance and petition for all the saints" (Eph. 6:18). We must always remember that the battle is not ours but God's. "Do not fear or be dismayed because of this great multitude, for the battle is not yours but God's" (2 Chron. 20:15). When you get the feeling that you are in the battle alone or that you cannot fight off Satan any longer, remember that the battle is not between you and some other person or even between you and Satan himself. The battle is bigger than that; it is between God and Satan, and you are only a participant. Because it is God's battle, continual, constant communication between you and God is essential.

The pattern of prayer is evident throughout the Bible from the time Adam communicated with God in the Garden, to Enoch walking with God, to Abraham praying on the way to sacrifice Issac, to the petitions of the psalmist, to the intercessions of the Hebrew prophets, to Jesus praying in the garden, to Paul praying that all Israel might be saved, to

John praying on Patmos. In no case did God delegate his role in prayer to another, not to an angel nor to a saint nor to a spirit; but he kept as his own the high privilege of prayerful communication with his people. If prayer is that important to God, we ought to practice its importance in our lives, not delegating to another the responsibility to pray for us, although their intercession is meaningful.

Prayer is asking God for what we desire. Jesus told his disciples, to "ask the Father for anything," (John 16:23), and Paul said, "Be anxious for nothing, but in everything by prayer and supplication with thanksgiving let your requests be made known to God" (Phil. 4:6). The response from God may not always be what we want, but it will always be in keeping with his will and for our best interests. So pray! Establish a disciplined prayer life so that you do not just pray when the mood hits you or the need overwhelms you. Pray spontaneously, as you go. However you do it, pray, for the battle is his, and communication is a must.

The relationship between you and the world is real. You can choose to withdraw from contact with non-Christians, but it will be difficult as well as unbiblical. The fight is real, but you have a real Lord who has provided you with real armor. Paul wrote, "I am no shadow-boxer, I really fight!" (1 Cor. 9:26, Phillips). Like Paul, fight the real enemy, Satan. Don't swing at your own shadow. View the non-Christian not as the enemy but as a friend and potential believer. And as you go, relate properly to the world.

For Further Study

Drumwright, Huber L. *Prayer Rediscovered.* Nashville: Broadman Press, 1978.

Fletcher, Jesse C. *Practical Discipleship.* Nashville: Broadman Press, 1980.

Haden, Ben. *Pray! Don't Settle for a Two-Bit Prayer Life.* Nashville: Thomas Nelson, Inc., 1974.

Jones, Russell Bradley. *A Survey of the Old and New Testaments.* Grand Rapids: Baker Book House, 1957.

Larson, Bruce. *Living on the Growing Edge.* Grand Rapids: Zondervan Publishing Co., 1968.

Little, Paul E. *Know What You Believe.* Wheaton Il.: Victor Books, 1970

Little, Paul E. *Know Why You Believe.* Downers Grove, Il.: Inter Varsity Press, 1968.
Ogilvie, Lloyd John. *Praying With Power.* Ventura, Ca.: Regal Books, 1983.
Rinker, Rosalind. *Conversational Prayer.* Waco: Word Books, Inc. 1970.
Rinker, Rosalind. *Prayer: Conversing With God.* Grand Rapids: Zondervan Publishing Co., 1959.
Stanley, Charles. *Handle With Prayer.* Wheaton, Il.: Victor Books, 1982.
Swindoll, Charles R. *Strengthening Your Grip: Essentials in an Aimless World.* Waco: Word Books, Inc. 1982.
Taylor, Jack. *Prayer: Life's Limitless Reach.* Nashville: Broadman Press, 1977.
Thompson, W. Oscar. *Concertric Circles of Concern.* Nashville: Broadman Press, 1981.

Note

1. For further elaboration on the redemptive outline of the Bible, see *A Survey of the Old and New Testaments,* Russell Bradley Jones.

6

The Verbalization
of EvangeLife

Naming the Name Above Every Name

There comes a time when the name above every name must be named. We can understand the importance of life-style evangelism—be in right relationship to God through his Word, worship him, and serve on his behalf; attempt to follow the model of Jesus Christ; allow the power of the Holy Spirit to work within and through us; and be in right relationship to the world—yet still not verbalize Jesus' name. To do all of the above and not name his name is to fall short of life-style evangelism. Indeed, if Jesus Christ is active in your life, he will show through. To refrain from identifying him verbally is to bear false witness.

If Jesus could not hide himself, what makes me think I can hide him in my life? On one occasion Jesus "went away to the region of Tyre. And when He had entered a house, He wanted no one to know of it; yet He could not escape notice" (Mark 7:24). The nonbelievers in his day seemed to always know where Jesus was. If he is allowed to be active in our lives, nonbelievers will likewise know where Jesus is. Likewise, the people of New Testament times could recognize his followers as they did Peter and John. "Now as they observed the confidence of Peter and John, . . . they were marveling, and began to recognize them as having been with Jesus" (Acts 4:13). If you and I will walk with Jesus and model after his example, our peers will take note of us also "as having been with Jesus." If he is active in our lives, we cannot hide him from public notice.

I have a tendency to talk about those things that are important in my life. If it is football season, I talk about the Dallas Cowboys and the University of Texas Longhorns. If it is baseball season, I talk about the

Atlanta Braves and, in June, the College World Series. In season and out of season, I talk about my family. I talk about my job and my church. These are items of importance to me, and they surface in my talk. When Jesus is real to me and I am following his model, I talk about him. One of the keys to verbalizing Jesus Christ is a daily relationship with him as part of my life-style. If he is important in my daily life, I cannot hide him from public notice.

There is a barrier to the verbalization of the good news of Jesus Christ. In spite of all the factors I would like to blame, the one barrier to my verbalization is myself. It just may be true, as it appears to be, that verbalization rises and falls with self-image. When I am confident of myself and my faith, I am more verbal about Christ. When I am unsure of myself and out of harmony with Christ, I do not talk about my faith as much. I have both experienced this personally and observed it in others. Let's explore it further.

The Barrier to Verbalization: Self

To explore self is to explore a complicated, yet challenging subject. True knowledge of self is possible only to the one who believes in God. In his "Essays on Man," Alexander Pope wrote, "Know thyself." Since persons are created in the image of God (Gen. 1:27), knowledge of self is only possible when we begin with knowledge of God. To know God is to know what we ought to be. To know self is to know that which keeps us from being what we ought to be. The barrier to verbalization of faith in Jesus Christ is self. The apostle Paul had a view of self that is worth noting.

Paul challenged us to think sober, balanced thoughts about ourselves. "For by the grace given me I say to every one of you: Do not think of yourself more highly than you ought, but rather think of yourself with sober judgment, in accordance with the measure of faith God has given you" (Rom. 12:3, NIV). The word *sober* has the meaning of being mentally balanced or having a sound mind. Those to whom Paul was writing had a problem of thinking of themselves too highly. As I travel around this country and meet many Christians, I am becoming increasingly convinced that this is not our problem. Whereas I have met some who think of themselves too highly, the vast majority of Christians today think too little of themselves. Since Paul used the word meaning "sober judgment" or mentally balanced, he implied that we were not to think thoughts of ourself that were too high or too low but balanced, sober thoughts of self.

Many Christians have a low self-image spiritually. When the call goes out for teachers in a church program, some people who might like to teach refuse because they don't think they have the proper training. When we invite persons to join the church choir, some people who may have a secret desire to sing don't because they have never had voice lessons. When the recruitment is made for workers in Vacation Bible School, many excuse themselves because they have never had any child psychology. The illustrations are endless. We do not respond in service because we are too busy putting ourselves down spiritually. When will we learn that God is not nearly as interested in our abilities as he is interested in our availability? The apostle Paul wrote that we should have balanced thoughts about ourselves. You are a creature made in the image of God with unlimited potential. God has a wonderful plan for your life regardless of your failures or successes. God's people are special to him. He both told us that and demonstrated it.

That which God said to the people of Israel has application to the "new Israel," the believers in Jesus Christ. One day God called to Moses from the mountain of Sinai and instructed him to tell the people—God's people —that they were God's special, treasured possessions. "If only you will now listen to me and keep my covenant, then out of all peoples you shall become my special possession; for the whole earth is mine" (Ex. 19:5, NEB). The *New International Version* says, "You will be my treasured possession." The word is *segula* and has an exciting meaning. In those days, the kings owned everything—the house in which you lived, the clothes which you wore, etc. When you own everything, what is special? Each king had, in his palace, a *segula*—a treasure chest of "special possessions" which might include a trophy of war or a gift from another king. It was his shoe box under the bed, to put it in our terminology. Special private possessions were kept in this treasure chest. The God who owns everything, whose brand is on the cattle on a thousand hills, whose copyright is on the bird's song—this great God said of his people, "You shall become my [*segula*] special [treasured] possession." You and I are special to God. We ought to act more like special possessions, especially in light of the New Testament demonstration of that specialness.

That which God promised on Sinai, he demonstrated on Calvary. The magnitude of God's love, the depth of his feeling for his own special possession, was demonstrated in the giving of his only Son to die on a cross. "For God loved the world so much that he gave his only Son, so that everyone who believes in him may not die but have eternal life" (John 3:16, GNB). Even though God demonstrated to us how special we are by magnifying Jesus on the cross, we allow Satan to magnify our selves. The result is excuses for not verbalizing our faith.

With self being the barrier to verbalization, the excuses are numerous. Perhaps the number one excuse for Christians not verbalizing their faith more than they do is the excuse of fear. We are afraid of rejection, of being made fun of, of questions we can't answer, of peer pressure, of a hundred things. We are afraid because people talk back. I'd fight the heavyweight champion of the world if he would agree not to fight back. I'd witness to everyone I met if they would agree not to talk back. But the world champion would not agree to that, nor would the non-Christian; so I must verbalize, knowing that they will talk back. That makes me afraid. But what is the real problem? Is it fear? "God hath not given us the spirit of fear; but of power, and of love, and of a sound mind" (2 Tim. 1:7, KJV). The real problem is self. We are afraid of what will happen to self—an embarrassment, a bruised ego, a strained relationship. A healthy self-image will go a long way in preventing fear from being an excuse for not verbalizing our faith.

There are other excuses for our lack of verbalization. Sometimes we excuse ourselves with misplaced priorities. We do so many good things, we just never get around to verbalizing. God has called us to be "ambassadors for Christ" (2 Cor. 5:20), but misplaced priorities make us secret agents instead. The problem is not misplaced priorities, it is self; for I set my own priorities, at least for the time that is my own. Some use prejudice as an excuse for lack of or limited verbalization. You might be prejudiced against methods—tracts or memorized outlines; prejudiced against motives, some of which you suspect are false; prejudiced against people, some of whom you'd rather not talk to. The real problem is not prejudice but self. You determine your own prejudices, so deal with them, and conquer them for the sake of verbalizing the good news.

Other excuses keep us from verbalizing. Some excuse themselves from verbalizing because their life-styles are not good enough. Perhaps they know that their life-styles do not live up to the verbal witness. That's one reason mission trips have been so popular. I can easily get a group of Christians to go across the country or to another country to share their faith in Christ. But getting them to share their faith where they live is tough. In the far away place, the non-Christian does not have the chance to compare my verbal witness with my life-style, so it is easy to witness verbally. The closer one gets to home the harder it is to witness verbally if the life-style and the verbal witness do not harmonize, and the most difficult place of all to share verbal witness is in the home where we are known best. But again, the real problem is not life-style but self. The answer may lie in improving your life-style, or it may lie in an awareness that you do not have to be perfect to share verbal witness. But nevertheless, you control your own life-style, thus self is the real barrier.

One pastor had said nothing in the hour we had been discussing a statewide effort in witness training for single adults. Of all the pastors present, he was the only silent participant. I worry about those kind. On this occasion my worries were justified, for when he did speak he dropped a verbal bomb on the planning sessions. His only question was, "How can you have the audacity to train single adults to witness when they have so many problems of their own?" I confess that I was momentarily without words. I couldn't believe the question. My answer could have been a bit more gentle had the question not been so blunt. My response was, "Jesus had problems, and I can name you twelve of them who followed him around, but it didn't stop him from witnessing." And that is the point! You don't wait until you are without problems to witness. You witness from your present life-style. Self says wait until things are better. The Scripture says "as you go" with no indication of a waiting period.

Still others excuse themselves from verbalization due to lack of assurance. With self as the real problem, you can deal with the lack of assurance by reading and applying 1 John 5:11-12: "God has given us eternal life, and this life is in His Son. He who has the Son has the life; he who does not have the Son of God does not have the life" (1 John 5:11-12). If you ever invited the Son of God, Jesus Christ, into your life, he is there to stay; and you can share him with others. If you have not invited him in, you can do so right now and begin to share him with others. Four times in Matthew's Gospel account, Jesus told his disciples that they had "little faith" (Matt. 6:30; 8:26; 16:8; 14:31), and each time it followed a failure on their part. Sometimes our faith is small. We can increase our faith through a renewed harmony with Jesus Christ. Whether the excuse is lack of faith or little faith, we control the excuse because self is the real barrier.

Each excuse we make for failing to verbalize our faith is directly related to the barrier of self. You and I must decide to witness in spite of self, if not in harmony with self. The Word, when verbalized, will not return void or empty (Isa. 55:11). And there is sufficient reason for our verbalization of the good news.

The Reason for Verbalization: Christ

Just as there is only one barrier to verbalization (self), there is only one reason for verbalization—Jesus Christ. He must be the motivation for verbalization; any other will be less than best. Some verbalize out of fear of not pleasing another person, some verbalize after the example of a respected friend, still others verbalize in the temporary excitement of a spiritual mountaintop experience. They verbalize best who verbalize out of the motivation provided by Jesus himself.

The work of Jesus is a reason for verbalization. If, before this day is over, someone dies for you, could you keep it a secret? Just suppose that another person, whether intentionally or not, died in your place today. You should have been killed, by all practical reasons, but another died instead. Could you go to work or to school or to church and not tell anyone about it? Could you sit through the next meal with your family and not breathe a word of it? I doubt if you could keep silent about something as meaningful as that. Yet, in spite of the fact that Jesus Christ died for us, we keep silent. Telling someone about the death of Jesus for us should be one of the most natural and enjoyable things we do. It seems to me we spend a great amount of time and energy making difficult that which God has made easy. Jesus not only died for us but also called us to be his witnesses.

The call of Jesus is another reason for verbalization. The last recorded words of Jesus to his disciples were, "You shall be My witnesses . . . to the remotest part of the earth" (Acts 1:8). That is not a multiple choice question or an optional extra. It is a statement of fact. If you are a Christian, you are a witness. You may be a good witness, a mediocre witness, a poor witness, or some other kind of witness. Whatever you do or say is a witness for Jesus Christ. His call assures us of that. Beyond his work and his call, Jesus and his followers set the example for verbalization.

The example of Jesus and his followers is a third reason for verbalization of the good news. We have already looked at the model of Jesus and seen his consistency in verbalizing the good news, but what of his followers? According to the Gospel of John, Andrew heard about Jesus from the preaching of John the Baptist. In the very next verse, John wrote of Andrew, "He found first his own brother Simon, and said to him, 'We have found the Messiah' (which translated means Christ). He brought him to Jesus" (John 1:41-42). When Jesus found Philip and instructed him to follow, it took John only two more verses to add, "Philip found Nathanael, and said to him, 'We have found Him of whom Moses in the Law and also the Prophets wrote, Jesus of Nazareth, the son of Joseph' " (John 1:45). After her own discovery, the woman of Samaria went into her village of Sychar from the well to say to the people, "Come, see a man who told me everything I ever did. Could this be the Christ?" (John 4:29, NIV). Those who first met Jesus set the example for us to begin immediately to verbalize our new discovery. But in addition to the work of Jesus, his call and the example left by his followers, the result of his life as experienced by you is a reason for verbalization of the good news to others who need to hear.

The result of Jesus as experienced by you is a fourth reason for verbalization. We had taxied out to the end of the runway of the Dallas/Fort Worth Airport on our way to New Orleans when a severe storm moved in over the runway. The pilot informed us that our flight would be delayed while we waited for the storm to pass. We sat on the end of the runway for one hour and forty minutes. It gave me ample time to talk with the passenger seated next to me, and I needed all of the time plus more.

My fellow passenger was a Jewish lawyer who had been educated at the Hebrew University in Jerusalem. While at the university, he had a "religious experience." As he said, "All the stories I had been told as a child came alive to me as I saw Jerusalem and studied there." As he shared with me about his Jewish faith, I shared with him about my Christian faith. One major problem with our discussion was his failure to accept Jesus as the fulfillment of his Old Testament faith and my failure to embrace the Hebrew faith minus the person of Jesus, seen as the promised Messiah.

Neither of us gained nor gave an inch in the long discussion. Both of us were impressed with the depth of commitment which was obvious in our personal experiences. His final word to me as we departed our much overdue jet in New Orleans was, "I do not accept your Jesus, but I accept you as a friend and appreciate your experience." As important as Jesus' work, his call, and his example are, there are those rare occasions when the life of Jesus as experienced by you and me will communicate with the greatest effectiveness. We must always remember that there are those who need to hear the good news verbalized by us, yet they may not believe in the reality of God or that Jesus Christ is the Son of God or in the authority of the Bible (or New Testament). Our personal experiences, hopefully supported by a committed life-style, will be our best verbalization. We have considered the barrier as well as the reason for verbalization. We must now turn to that which we are to verbalize.

The Ingredients of Verbalization: The Gospel

In addition to verbalizing what God has done for us in Jesus Christ, we need to verbalize what we know God can do for others. This knowledge comes to us not only from our own experience but also from God's Word, the Bible. There is a plan of salvation set forth in the Bible for us to verbalize. Even though we give to this plan our own terminology at times, we must be careful not to insist on all people responding with our exact terminology. It is possible for someone else to become a Christian without using the same words that you used when you became a Christian. The plan is the same; the words may differ. Out of my own Christian heritage, I use the following words to describe the biblical plan for obtaining new life, salvation.

The first ingredient of verbalization is God's love and care for all persons. The Bible begins with the God of love. Jesus said in his prayer to God, "You loved me before the creation of the world" (John 17:24, NIV). Before God ever created, he loved. Out of this love, he created all things, including humanity as the object of his love (Gen. 1:1-31). We have already seen that God loved the world so much that he "gave His only begotten Son, that whoever believes in Him should not perish, but have eternal life" (John 3:16). Jesus further emphasized this when he said, "I came that they might have life, and might have it abundantly" (John 10:10). It is good that God loves us, for sin has put us in need of his love.

The second ingredient of verbalization is humanity's sinfulness. It is best to begin with God's love, for most people will listen out of their own desire to be loved. To begin with sin is to risk not getting to your second point. To omit sin is to leave the plan incomplete. So you should emphasize that "all have sinned" (Rom. 3:23) and that "all of us like sheep have gone astray" (Isa. 53:6). Having identified yourself as one with the sinful person, you are free to identify that person as having sinned. Tell him or her as did Isaiah, "It is because of your sins that he doesn't hear you. It is your sins that separate you from God when you try to worship him" (Isa. 59:2, GNB). Since "there is no one who does not sin" (2 Chron. 6:36, GNB), he or she is included in Paul's statement, "For the wages of sin is death, but the free gift of God is eternal life in Christ Jesus our Lord" (Rom. 6:23). Whereas there is no graceful way to tell people that they are sinners, by identifying with them you can show them how you found forgiveness and release in the person of Jesus Christ.

The third ingredient of verbalization is the person and work of Jesus Christ. Wherever you begin in the verbalization of the plan, go straight to the person and work of Jesus. The non-Christian needs to know that "God demonstrates His own love toward us, in that while we were yet sinners, Christ died for us" (Rom. 5:8) and that "because of our sins he was given over to die, and he was raised to life in order to put us right with God" (Rom. 4:25, GNB). Your friends who refuse to accept the New Testament need to know that it was "because of our sins he was wounded, beaten because of the evil we did. We are healed by the punishment he suffered, made whole by the blows he received" (Isa. 53:5, GNB). Jesus said, "I am the resurrection and the life; he who believes in Me shall live even if he dies, and everyone who lives and believes in Me shall never die" (John 11:25-26), and again, "I am the way, and the truth, and the life; no one comes to the Father, but through Me" (John 14:6). The non-Christian needs to know that "by the death of Christ we are set free, that is, our sins are forgiven" (Eph. 1:7, GNB). Part of your verbalization will be offering and encouraging a time of response on the part of the non-Christian.

The fourth ingredient of verbalization is humanity's response in repentance, confession, and faith. Inform the non-Christian, "If you confess with your mouth Jesus as Lord, and believe in your heart that God raised Him from the dead, you shall be saved" (Rom. 10:9-10). Jesus instructed those who would follow him to "repent ['turn away from,' GNB]" (Mark 1:15). John wrote, "If we confess our sins, He is faithful and righteous to forgive us our sins and to cleanse us from all unrighteousness" (1 John 1:9). Isaiah encouraged those Old Testament believers to "seek the Lord while He may be found; Call upon Him while He is near" (Isa. 55:6). The result of response is, "As many as received Him, to them He gave the right to become children of God, even to those who believe on His name" (John 1:12). Having verbalized concerning a response, the decision is up to the non-Christian listener.

The fifth ingredient to verbalization is humanity's decision. The biblical record is clear when it says, "Believe in the Lord Jesus, Christ, and you shall be saved" (Acts 16:31). It is the picture of Jesus standing at the door of a life and knocking, saying, "If anyone hears My voice and opens the door, I will come in to him" (Rev. 3:20). You must press gently for a decision that is real. The answer is not true or false but yes or no. The decision does not call merely for intellectual assent but for a commitment of life. If the response of the non-Christian is a negative one, you should seek clarification. Be sure the person understood your presentation. Probe gently, but do not push. Leave the door open for whoever might be used of God to verbalize the gospel to that person next. If the non-Christian's response is positive, lead him or her to invite Jesus Christ into his or her life and begin the follow-through.

The sixth ingredient to verbalization is follow-through. Jesus instructed his disciples not only to make disciples but to baptize them and teach them "to observe all that I have commanded you" (Matt. 28:20). As a prelude to their own life-style of evangelism, new Christians will need to know that they have now been "crucified with Christ; and it is no longer I who live, but Christ who lives in me; and the life I now live in the flesh I live by faith in the Son of God, who loved me, and delivered Himself up for me" (Gal. 2:20). The apostle Paul believed in follow-through. Either he followed through himself or assigned the task to another or wrote letters back to the new converts. How you follow through is not as important as the fact that you do follow through. Can you imagine someone giving birth to a newborn baby, then leaving the hospital with a wish for the baby's well-being? Neither should you be a part of the spiritual birthing process only to walk off and leave the newborn believer to grow up on his own.

I challenge you to begin to think positivly about your verbalizing of the good news. Too much time is wasted on developing excuses, all of which relate to the same barrier of self. Begin to think of the positive response that will be made by non-Christians as you verbalize your faith. My friend Fred Akers, head football coach at the University of Texas, told me how he motivated his players. He asks the entire team to picture in their minds what it will be like in the winning locker room after the game and how they will celebrate their victory. He specifically asks the running backs to picture what it will be like to break through the line and dash into the end zone for a touchdown and asks the wide receivers to picture catching a pass for a first down and asks the defensive linemen to picture sacking the opposing quarterback for a big loss on third down, and so on through the team. By the time the game starts, the players have already tasted victory so much that they are determined to win. This positive planning will work in verbalizing our faith. We need to begin picturing in our minds the positive response people will make to our witness. Begin now to celebrate the victory of new life in Christ on behalf of a non-Christian.

Life-style evangelism does begin with your basic relationship to God and continues as you model after Jesus Christ in the power of the Holy Spirit, related to a non-Christian world, but don't forget to verbalize the good news—expect positive results. There comes a time when the Name above every name must be named. As you go . . . verbalize!

For Further Study

Autrey, C. E. *You Can Win Souls.* Nashville: Broadman Press, 1961.

Brooks, Hal. *Follow Up Evangelism.* Nashville: Broadman Press, 1972.

Eims, Leroy. *Winning Ways.* Wheaton, Il.: Victor Books, 1974.

Eims, Leroy. *What Every Christian Should Know About Growing.* Wheaton, Il.: Victor Books, 1976.

Ford, Leighton. *Good News is for Sharing.* Elgin, Il.: David C. Cook Publishing Co., 1977.

Hanks, Billie. *Everyday Evangelism.* Grand Rapids: Zondervan Publishing Co., 1983.

Havlik, John. *People Centered Evangelism.* Nashville: Broadman Press, 1973.

Hogue, C. B. *The Doctrine of Salvation.* Nashville: Convention Press, 1978.

Kennedy, D. James. *Evangelism Explosion.* Wheaton, Il.: Tyndale House, 1970.

Little, Paul E. *How to Give Away Your Faith.* Downers Grove, Il.: Inter Varsity Press, 1966.

Matthews, C. E., revised by C. B. Hogue and Roy T. Edgemon. *Every Christian's Job.* Nashville: Convention Press, 1951, 1980.

Moore, Waylon B. *New Testament Follow Up.* Grand Rapids: Wm. B. Eerdmans Co., 1963.

Neighbour, Ralph W., Jr. *Survival Kit for New Christians.* Nashville: Convention Press, 1979.

Read, David H. C. *Go & Make Disciples.* Nashville: Abingdon Press, 1978.

Rinker, Rosalind. *You Can Witness With Confidence.* Grand Rapids: Zondervan Publishing House, 1962.

Smith, Bailey E. *Real Evangelism: Exposing the Subtle Substitutes for That Evangelism.* Nashville: Broadman Press, 1978.

Worrell, George E. *How to Take the Worry Out of Witnessing.* Nashville: Broadman Press, 1976.

7

The Support System of EvangeLife

The Body of Christ

Of extreme importance in a life-style of evangelism is the support system which we know as the church, the body of Christ. When the apostle Paul likened the church to marriage, he was referring to a relationship of support and complement. Just as wives are to be subject to their husbands, so ought the church to be subject to Christ, its Head (Eph. 5:22-23). Paul said Christ loved the church and gave himself for her (Eph. 5:25) and wants the church to be "pure and faultless, without spot or wrinkle or any other imperfection" (Eph. 5:27, GNB). But Paul also said, "we are members of His body" (Eph. 5:30), the church, and as members we ought to love the church.

I am a product of the church. I grew up in a parsonage, son of a Baptist pastor. I cut my first teeth on a Broadman hymnal in the back pew of a country church in central Texas. I grew up in the church. The great majority of my treasured memories of childhood and my teenage years relate to church activities. I became a Christian as the result of conviction first felt at a church camp. I was baptized in the church. I felt my first call to Christian ministry at a statewide summer assembly in Palacios, Texas. I was licensed to preach by a church. I attended a church-supported college and while there, met and married my wife who had also been raised in the church. I was ordained to the gospel ministry at the request of a church which had called me to be their pastor. I have served as pastor of two churches, interim pastor of many, supply preacher in many more. For fifteen years, I served as an employee of the Baptist General Convention of Texas; now as a national consultant for the Southern Baptist Home

Mission Board, I work with churches all over the United States. I am a product of the church, and I love the church, but I am greatly concerned about its well-being.

We need to support the church and to be supported by the church. Since the church is made up of people, I am saying we need to support people and be supported by people, as well as support related to the institution. Yet what I am seeing, with obvious exceptions, is a strong desire to "do my own thing," to march to my own drummer, to cut my own path. That which happens among the churches also happens within the local church. Individualism has its place, but its place is not first. "I did it my way" was a popular song but it is not a hymn, nor is it biblical. We must do it God's way, and God's way is through the church as a support system of fellow believers. It breaks my church-oriented heart to see quarreling and fighting among the churches and within church memberships when we, of all people, should be supporting each other, in spite of our differences. We need a rediscovery of the concept discussed by the apostle Paul in Romans 12.

The Proper Relationship to the Body of Christ

There is both unity and diversity in our relationship to the body of Christ. Paul wrote, "Just as each of us has one body with many members, and these members do not all have the same function, so in Christ we who are many form one body, and each member belongs to all the others. We have different gifts, according to the grace given us" (Rom. 12:4-6, NIV).

As to the unity involved in our relationship to the body of Christ, Paul said we are "one body." The parallel is made to the human body. My body is one body and is a united body. All the members of my body are connected. To accept the body is to accept all of its parts, and to reject the body is to reject all of its parts. I am like a star with many points. Some of those points are sharp while others are blunt; some are bright while others are dull; some are broad while others are narrow; some are beautiful while others are ugly, but all my points are connected. Accept me, and you accept all of me; reject me, and you reject all of me. Likewise with the body of Christ, for it is "one body." In 1 Corinthians 12:15-21, Paul mentioned various members of the human body—foot, hand, ear, eye,

nose, head—yet he concluded, "There should be no division in the body
. . . you are Christ's body, and individually members of it" (1 Cor.
12:25-27).

As to the diversity involved in your relationship to the body of Christ,
Paul said the "one body" (v. 12) has "many members" (v. 12) and "variet-
ies of gifts" (v. 4). Although all the parts of my body are connected—
united—they are not all equal, nor are any of them a majority. Each
member of my body has it's own function. If my ear decides that it no
longer wants to hear and out of its jealousy demands to see, how will I
hear? And if the ear starts seeing, obviously not as good as the eye can
see, the eyes may get fed up and refuse to function any longer. Now my
body must function with no hearing and limited sight. Eventually other
members of the body get upset, and their various reactions further upset
the unity. Sounds like some churches doesn't it? That's the point! The
church is not to be that way, for "God himself has put the body together
. . . so there is no division in the body, but all its different parts have the
same concern for one another" (1 Cor. 12:24-25, GNB).

With many members and different gifts, the church must function with
its diversity. Just as there are no majority parts to my physical body, there
are no majority gifts in the spiritual body. But with our different gifts, we
function as a unity. Each part of the body is crucial to the overall functioning of the body; and whereas not all the parts are seen, all are important.
Paul indicated that we see the members of the body differently, but "God
has combined the members of the body and has given greater honor to the
parts that lacked it, so that there should be no division in the body" (1
Cor. 12:24-25, NIV). We must discover a balance to the unity and diversity of the body.

As to the balance involved in your relationship to the body of Christ,
the proper relationship comes when each member understands his own
spiritual gifts and appreciates the spiritual gifts of others. When I was
fifteen years old, I was in an automobile accident, and my neck was broken
at the second vertebra. Because I was not killed or paralyzed, as others
had been with the same injury, the doctors did not know what to do
with me.

For nine months, I was a medical experiment. Numerous times during those months, things were done to my body that upset the balance. The bone began to heal, then stopped healing. Surgery was planned, then canceled. A body cast was made for me, then discarded. Parts of my body ceased to function properly because the neck and its supporting muscles were not functioning. It was only after complete healing and rehabilitation that my whole body functioned again as a united body. I have a feeling that parts of my body learned to appreciate other parts of my body as they came to a greater awareness of their own function. If in the body of Christ we could understand our own gifts/function and begin to appreciate the gifts/function of others, we would have discovered a balance and our life-style of evangelism would not only be more effective but more acceptable by the observing world.

Discovering Your Connection to the Body: Spiritual Gifts

Because spiritual gifts have often been misunderstood and misapplied, they have frequently been overlooked. Growing up a Southern Baptist, I do not remember hearing much about spiritual gifts even in college and seminary courses. We have traditionally been afraid of that which we do not understand and which a few misuse. Fortunately, I crossed paths with a non-Southern Baptist who began to teach me about this powerful part of the New Testament. Lately, I have seen more and more articles and books on spiritual gifts authored by Southern Baptists and other Evangelicals who heretofore had either ignored or taken lightly this aspect of the church. My own feeling is that if a healthy concept of spiritual gifts ever breaks loose in evangelical churches it will be something to behold. Many will cooperate much better, and the entire body will be built up in a greater way then ever before. But before that happens, questions will have to be answered related to spiritual gifts.

The first question related to spiritual gifts is, Where do spiritual gifts come from? There is only one answer: spiritual gifts come from God. The church cannot bestow spiritual gifts on a member nor can the pastor or any other believer. God alone gives spiritual gifts.

A second question is, Where are spiritual gifts mentioned in the Bible? There are three lists of gifts in the New Testament—Romans 12:4-8; 1 Corinthians 12; Ephesians 4:1-16—and numerous other places where only one or two gifts are mentioned. Since the three lists are different, we may conclude that none of them is meant to be an exclusive list. Depending upon which writer/scholar you choose to believe, there are more than thirty spiritual gifts identified in the New Testament. There is vast disagreement over the validity of some of these gifts. Just the twenty-one gifts mentioned in Acts bring on much discussion and disagreement.

A third question is, What exactly is a spiritual gift? In his book *Your Spiritual Gifts Can Help Your Church Grow,* Peter Wagner offers this definition: "A spiritual gift is the special attribute given by the Holy Spirit to every believer according to God's grace for use within the context of the body."[1] Ralph Neighbour, Jr., describes spiritual gifts as "specific capacities produced in us by the entrance of the Holy Spirit . . . so that I might perform adequately as a member of Christ's body."[2]

Two related questions concerning spiritual gifts are: who has spiritual gifts? and why should that person try to discover what they are in her life? According to the New Testament, only believers in Jesus Christ have spiritual gifts. The conversion experience and the accompanying activation of the Holy Spirit in the new life bring about spiritual gifts. The discovery of that gift (or those gifts) may come much later as the new Christian matures in the faith and is introduced to the concept. Spiritual gifts must be discovered since they are given rather than earned and since they cannot be very well developed until their presence is known to the believer. There is some disagreement as to whether all the gifts a believer is to receive are given at conversion or if they are given as she matures in the faith. That is a disagreement that will continue for only God knows the answer. Either we get all that God has for us at conversion and discover it as we grow or we get the gifts as we grow. The issue is secondary to the discovery and use of the gifts.

Although there are other questions, the final question for consideration here is, What is the proper view of spiritual gifts? It is at this very point that some have misapplied the concept of spiritual gifts, and possibly this very misapplication that has caused others to de-emphasize the gifts. To have a spiritual gift and focus on or worship the gift rather than the Giver of the gift, God, is a sophisticated kind of idolatry. Anything that is worshiped in the place of God—spiritual gifts, a building, a pastor or evangelist, a version of the Bible, a time of day—is idolatry. Some idolatry is not as easily identified since it has the appearance of being spiritual. We must keep the focus on the Giver of the gifts and let the gifts themselves be seen and used in the proper perspective. Since God gives believers just what he wants them to have, it is wrong for me to desire or demand a certain gift for you. But for me to encourage you to be in a right relationship to God and thereby understand and use your spiritual gift is both right and desirable. Keep your focus on God, and your gift will be revealed and applied properly.

There are no simple ways suggested for you to discover your spiritual gifts. Perhaps an elimination of certain things sometimes mistaken for gifts will help. Spiritual gifts and fruit of the Spirit are not the same. The fruit of the Spirit listed in Galatians 5:22-23 are to be produced in every believer's life whereas various gifts are given selectively through God's grace. Nor should spiritual gifts be mistaken for talents. Although God may well give you a gift in harmony with your talent, it is not the same. Playing baseball well is for some people a talent, yet it is not a spiritual gift. A non-Christian may have a real talent for public speaking, become a Christian, and discover that his spiritual gift is exhortation or teaching but may just as easily become a Christian and discover some other spiritual gift. Talents and gifts are not the same. Some may mistake spiritual gifts for counterfeit gifts. Suffice it to say on this subject that whatever God has that is working, Satan tries to get in on it, and apparently God allows Satan certain limited abilities to do so.

One major misunderstanding comes in the area of Christian responsibilities or temporary tasks. The church of which I am a member, Smoke Rise Baptist Church in Stone Mountain, Georgia, as well as the last church of which I was a member, Hyde Park Baptist Church in Austin, Texas—voted to build a new auditorium. In both cases, I not only voted for it but pledged to give an amount of money beyond my regular offering toward the costs of building the auditorium. Although I do not have to the best of my understanding the spiritual gift of giving, I assumed a responsibility or temporary task of giving. I accomplished that task through a commitment and through discipline while others with the gift of giving gave freely and naturally. Another example would be in the spiritual gift of celibacy which the apostle Paul said he had (1 Cor. 7:7-8). Christians suffer the loss of their mates through death. Do they then have the gift of celibacy? I think not, or they probably would not have married in the first place. Rather they now have a new-found Christian responsibility of celibacy that may or may not be temporary, depending on their future remarriage to someone else or their continued widowhood. Do not confuse a spiritual gift with a Christian responsibility or temporary task.

Possible spiritual gifts should be tested, if at all practical. If you believe you have the gift of teaching, you ought to teach. If everyone goes to sleep as you teach, you might try another gift which you believe you have. Often other Christians will see the gift in you before you discover it. Spiritual gifts should be affirmed by fellow believers and confirmed by trusted Christian friends. If you are the only person who thinks you have a particular gift, you may be mistaken. It was an exciting time for me as a young minister, even before understanding spiritual gifts, to try certain things. Those faithful folk whom I pastored kept telling me they enjoyed my teaching. Years later, I was delighted to discover that I had a teaching gift. In fact, my discoveries have shown that God's gifts to me have been in those areas where I enjoy serving and in those areas where I function more naturally. I can function in other areas and have done so with some degree of success, but it has taken much more commitment and discipline. The excitement of testing spiritual gifts is exceeded only by the excitement of discovery and implementation.

Perhaps it would be helpful to list some of the more widely agreed upon spiritual gifts with Scripture references so that you can begin to study, test, and discover your own spiritual gift. As I offer this list, I honor your right to add to the list gifts which you feel I have omitted or omit from the list gifts which you feel should not be listed. This is a representative list and not meant to be exhaustive:

Prophecy/Preaching: 1 Corinthians 12:10; Ephesians 4:11-14; Romans 12:6; Luke 7:26; Acts 15:32; Acts 21:9-11

Pastoring/Shepherding: Ephesians 4:11-14; 1 Timothy 3:1-7; John 10:1-8; 1 Peter 5:1-3

Teaching: 1 Corinthians 12:28; Ephesians 4:11-14; Romans 12:7; Acts 18:24-28; Acts 20:20-21

Wisdom: 1 Corinthians 2:1-13; 1 Corinthians 12:8; Acts 6:3,10; James 1:5-6; 2 Peter 3:15

Knowledge/Insight: 1 Corinthians 2:14; 1 Corinthians 12:8; Acts 5:1-11; Colossians 2:2-3; 2 Corinthians 11:6

Exhortation/Encouragement: Romans 12:8; 1 Timothy 4:13; Hebrews 10:25; Acts 14:22

Distinguishing/Discerning of Spirits: 1 Corinthians 12:10; Acts 5:1-11; Acts 16:16-18; 1 John 4:1-6; Matthew 16:21-23

Giving: Romans 12:8; 2 Corinthians 8:1-7; 2 Corinthians 9:2-8; Mark 12:41-44

Helping/Assisting: 1 Corinthians 12:28; Romans 16:1-2; Acts 9:36; Luke 8:2-3; Mark 15:40-41

Mercy/Kindness: Romans 12:8; Mark 9:41; Acts 16:33-34; Luke 10:33-35; Matthew 25:34-40; Matthew 20:29-34; Acts 11:28-30

Missionary: 1 Corinthians 9:19-23; Acts 8:4; Acts 13:2-4a; Acts 22:21; Romans 10:14-15

Evangelism: Ephesians 4:11-14; 2 Timothy 4:5; Acts 8:5-6; Acts 14:21; Acts 21:8

Hospitality: 1 Peter 4:9; Romans 12:9-13; Romans 16:23; Acts 16:14-15; Hebrews 13:1-2

Faith: 1 Corinthians 12:9; Acts 11:22-24; Acts 27:21-25; Hebrews 11; Romans 4:18-21

Leadership: 1 Timothy 5:17; Acts 7:10; Acts 15:7-11; Romans 12:8; Hebrews 13:17; Luke 9:51

Administration/Direction: 1 Corinthians 12:28; Acts 6:1-7; Acts 27:11; Luke 14:28-30

Apostle/Messenger: 1 Corinthians 12:28; 2 Corinthians 12:12; Ephesians 4:11-14; Ephesians 3:1-9; Acts 15:1-2; Galatians 2:7-10

Celibacy: 1 Corinthians 7:7-8; Matthew 19:10-12

Intercession: James 5:14-16; 1 Timothy 2:1-2; Colossians 1:9-12; Colossians 4:12-13; Acts 12:12; Luke 22:41-44

Service/Ministry: 2 Timothy 1:16-18; Romans 12:7; Acts 6:1-7; Titus 3:14; Galatians 6:2,10

We must now focus on how to use your spiritual gifts in life-style evangelism. Those who have spent far more years than I studying and surveying spiritual gifts estimate that only 5 percent or less or all believers have the gift of evangelism. Before you sigh relief, let me remind you that 100 percent of all believers have the commission to witness (Matt. 28:19-20). Most will not have the gift of evangelism. If you do not, does that mean you don't have to witness? No! It means that for you to witness, it will take a little more of a commitment to it and the employment of some spiritual discipline. You can become as effective a witness as the gifted evangelist, but it will come through commitment and discipline rather than coming naturally as it will for the gifted evangelist.

The purpose of spiritual gifts is the "building up of the body of Christ" (Eph. 4:12). There are two ways to build up a body—internally and externally. We build up the body of Christ internally as we use our gifts to minister to each other and support each other. It is this to which Paul wrote, "Its parts should have equal concern for each other. If one part suffers, every part suffers with it; if one part is honored, every part rejoices with it" (1 Cor. 12:25-26, NIV). But we also build up the body externally as we add to it. Spiritual gifts are to be used within the context of the body. The New Testament references to spiritual gifts are addressed to the church, not to individuals. But part of that use within the context of the body is to assist each other in adding to the body. Jack MacGorman says, "Through the . . . gifts a church is equipped to function as a worshipping and witnessing community."[3] It is this "witnessing community" to which we need to give attention.

I know two women who have the spiritual gift of hospitality. At a suggestion of how to use their gifts in evangelism, they held a dessert party in their apartment complex and invited a lot of people to attend. On the night of the party, they had a crowd, a confirmation of their gift. You enjoy going into the home of one who has the spiritual gift of hospitality. During the party, one of the women stopped the proceedings long enough to share with the guests why they had been invited, related to the gift of hospitality. Everyone had such a good time that the women repeated the party occasionally. Within a week of the first party an international student living in the apartment complex had become a Christian, and he was followed by several others who professed faith in Christ as a result of the use of a spiritual gift by these two women. Although both readily admitted that they did not know how to witness, they faithfully used the gift God had given them, and he blessed their faithfulness. Not everyone has the gift of evangelism, but every believer has a gift or gifts. These gifts are to be used for the "building up of the body of Christ" as these women used their gift. Few things could be more natural in the life-style of a Christian than the natural use of spiritual gifts.

The apostle Paul wrote, "Now concerning spiritual gifts, brethren, I do not want you to be unaware" (1 Cor. 12:1). Neither do I want you to be unaware of this tremendous, effective method of bearing witness through both your life and your verbalization. Don't cut off your support system, rather relate to it through using your spiritual gifts and appreciating and affirming the gifts of other members of the body. And as you go, use your spiritual gifts, indeed your entire support system, in evangelizing.

For Further Study

Bridge, Donald and Phypers, David. *Spiritual Gifts and the Church.* Downers Grove, Il.: Inter Varsity Press, 1973.

Flynn, Leslie, B. *Nineteen Gifts of the Spirit.* Wheaton, Il.: Victor Books, 1974.

Green, Michael. *Evangelism Now & Then.* Downers Grove, Il.: Inter Varsity Press, 1979.

Griffiths, Michael. *Grace-Gifts.* Grand Rapids: Wm. B. Eerdmans Publishing Co., 1978.

MacGorman, Jack W. *The Gifts of the Spirit.* Nashville: Broadman Press, 1974.

Marney, Carlyle. *Priests to Each Other.* Valley Forge, Pa.: Judson Press, 1974.

McNair, Jim. *Love & Gifts.* Minneapolis, Mn.: Bethany Fellowship, Inc., 1976.

Murphy, Edward F. *Spiritual Gifts and the Great Commission.* South Pasadena, Ca.: Mandate Press, 1975.

Neighbour, Ralph W., Jr. *This Gift is Mine.* Nashville: Broadman Press, 1974.

O'Conner, Elizabeth. *Eighth Day of Creation.* Waco: Word Books, Inc., 1971.

Richards, Lawrence O. and Martin, Gib. *A Theology of Personal Ministry: Giftedness in the Local Church.* Grand Rapids: Zondervan Publishing House, 1981.

Stedman, Ray C. *Body Life.* Ventura, Ca.: Regal Books, 1972.

Wagner, C. Peter. *Your Spiritual Gifts Can Help Your Church Grow.* Ventura, Ca.: Regal Books, 1979.

Yohn, Rick. *Discover Your Spiritual Gift and Use It.* Wheaton, Il.: Tyndale House Publishers, 1982.

Notes

1. C. Peter Wagner, *Your Spiritual Gifts Can Help Your Church Grow* (Ventura, CA: Regal Books, 1979), p.42

2. Ralph W. Neighbour, Jr., *This Gift Is Mine* (Nashville: Broadman Press, 1974), p.20.

3. J. W. MacGorman, *The Gifts of the Spirit* (Nashville: Broadman Press, 1974), p.32.

8

The Continuation of EvangeLife

Developing a Personal Strategy

A personal strategy of life-style evangelism will lead to success, whereas the lack of a strategy may lead to failure. I was in San Juan, Puerto Rico, for a meeting of the state evangelism directors. Following the first evening session, on Tuesday, a friend and I walked to an ice-cream parlor about three blocks from our hotel. On the way back to the hotel, we were approached by two very attractive women and asked if we needed any company. We quickly refused and crossed the street toward our hotel, laughing about the whole scene. On the second night of the meeting as I walked back from the ice-cream parlor, one of the same young women approached me and again asked if I wanted company for the evening. I again refused and made my way quickly back to the hotel. During that night I did not sleep well. I kept thinking about the boldness of the young woman who had twice approached me without any reservation. I also thought about my own failure to even share with her why I did not desire her company, not to mention my failure to share with her the most important news of Jesus Christ's love for her. The next morning I discovered that during the night a woman had been shot and killed in front of our hotel. I had no way of knowing if it were the same woman who had approached me, but I will forever live with a question and with a reminder of failure. Inside the hotel we were discussing strategy for evangelizing America, while outside people were dying and some of them going to hell. My failure to personally apply the strategy still haunts me. The New Testament has a strategy for evangelizing the world. We must make it personal, even when we fail.

Continuation when Your EvangeLife Fails

Those of us who speak and write know that for every success story we share we have about ten failure stories that we do not share. Sharing our failures makes us vulnerable, and we would rather not run the risk. The truth is that you will experience more failure than success. Let's define our terms. Success is when, given the opportunity, you share your testimony and God's plan of salvation. Failure is when, given the opportunity, you do not share your testimony or God's plan of salvation. My failure in San Juan was not the woman's failure to accept my message; it was my not sharing the message. The New Testament offers help. The writer of Hebrews wrote:

> Therefore, since we have so great a cloud of witnesses surrounding us, let us also lay aside every encumbrance, and the sin which so easily entangles us, and let us run with endurance the race that is set before us, fixing our eyes on Jesus, the author and perfector of faith, who for the joy set before Him endured the cross, despising the shame, and has sat down at the right hand of the throne of God (Heb. 12:1-2).

In these verses, the writer identified some reasons for failure. There are some "encumbrances" or weights that easily trip us up. In the athletic games of that day, as well as in the modern equivalent, runners would warm up with weights around their ankles so that, when the race began and they stripped off the weights, they would run lighter and faster. Running uniforms are made of the lightest possible material so that nothing will slow the runner. Warm-up suits are shed prior to the race, having served their purpose.

Do you know any Christians who are still trying to "run the race" with their warm-up suits on or with weights still around their ankles? We sometimes memorize a verbal presentation of the gospel in order to help us in witnessing. At a point of development in your life, you should take the basic facts of that verbalization and personalize it to your life and to the needs of the nonbeliever. Shed the weight of a memorized approach in favor of the freedom of a personalized presentation. There are other weights or "encumbrances" which you need to shed. Why not make a list and begin to work on them?

In addition to "encumbrances," the writer instructed us to lay aside "the sin which so easily entangles us" (v.1). This is a reference to the sin of unbelief, according to most New Testament scholars. Can you imagine a runner who did not believe that he could run the race well? In all probability, he would not run the race well. Can you imagine a runner beginning to doubt his abilities or the instructions of his coach or the safety of the track surface? Once doubt and unbelief set in, the race is hindered. Doubts will come, but they need not stay. Perhaps you will doubt your own conversion experience or some portion of the Bible or God's ability to work in and through you or the real lostness of non believers or some other aspect of your faith. Deal with your doubts, stand firm on your Christian beliefs, and run well the race set before you.

One of the solutions for failure mentioned by the writer of Hebrews is "run with endurance" (v. 1) or patience. The real idea is *stickability* although I don't think that is a word. Once you have begun the race—the Christian life—stay with it. Sure, times will be tough, and victory will not always be visible, but remain in the race. Or as a former coach of mine used to say, "Hang in there!" That's the idea. You do not quit because you fail in evangelism; you patiently try again and again with your focus in the right place.

The other solution mentioned by the writer of Hebrews is "fixing our eyes on Jesus" (v. 2). When we spend too much time focusing on our failure, we fail again. Focus on Jesus! Runners are trained to fix their eyes on an object and run toward that object. In a dash a runner will fix his eyes on the finish line and run toward it. In a long race, a runner will fix his eyes on some object and run toward it, finding a new object when the first one is passed and so on until the finish line is in sight. Likewise in the Christian faith, we must keep our eyes fixed on Jesus. Can you imagine what would happen to a runner if he began to look at the spectators or at the other runners or behind him to see who was catching up? You know he would probably fail or at least fail to perform at his best. The Christian life-style is best lived with your eyes on Jesus, not on someone or something else.

Eyes fixed on Jesus was a secret of success learned by the disciples. Have you thought about the diversity of that group? You would not want to be chairperson of that committee. Simon Peter, a former fisherman, was loud and sometimes obnoxious. When Jesus asked a question, Peter always answered first. That could get old in a group. John was a quiet, meditative man who, when Jesus asked a question, would like to have had a week to think about his answer. Peter and John were opposites, yet they worked side by side for the evangelization of the world. Thomas doubted most things and demanded proof on such things as the bodily resurrection of Jesus. Andrew, a man of untroubled faith, believed everything to the extent that he was almost gullible. That which Thomas doubted Andrew accepted without question, yet these two opposites worked side by side for the spreading of the good news. Simon the Zealot was a revolutionary whose group proposed the overthrow of the Roman government. Matthew had been a tax collector for the Roman government. That for which Matthew had stood Simon was out to destroy, yet these opposites worked side by side in witness. What was the secret of these early disciples? They stopped looking at each other long enough to look together at Jesus, and it will work for some other groups as well. Fix your eyes on Jesus, and the "race" will run amazingly well for victory will be in sight.

Continuation Assured of Victory

Whereas the writer of Hebrews likened the Christian life to a race that is run, there are two aspects of Christian life that are not like a race. One is the place of victory in the race and in the Christian life. If you were going to run a race, your purpose would relate to victory, either over the other competitors or over your own best time. In the Christian life, victory is not something we strive for because it is assured. Victory has already been won through the death and resurrection of Jesus Christ. We "run" not in order to win but because we have already won. With assurance of victory in mind, I wonder why there is so much competition among the runners. Relax, run well your race, live well your life, and the world will take notice as you run.

A second aspect of the Christian life that is not like a race relates to the importance of today. In a physical race, you know the exact location of the finish line and how far you need to go to reach it. The end is predetermined and fixed. In the Christian life, we are certain of a finish line, but we are uncertain as to its location in our life. Thus today is important.

Completing the round of golf, each member of the foursome commented as to how much fun it had been playing together, and we agreed to do it again. The occasion was the annual Texas Baptist Student Directors Seminar. As I totaled up the scores, I looked at four names on a scorecard— Dan, Ron, Chet, Don. Three months from that May afternoon Chet Reames, director of the Division of Student Work for the Baptist General Convention of Texas, was killed in an automobile accident. Shortly after that day Don Anthony, director of the Christian Education Coordinating Board for Texas Baptists was discovered to have terminal cancer and died the day after Thanksgiving. After both friends had died, Ron Durham and I reflected on the unbelievable fact that two men in their mid-forties could enjoy a round of golf in good health, yet six months later both be dead. No one could have predicted such an early finish line, nor can you predict your own finish line. Some run long races while others run short races. The importance is not in how long you run but in how well you run today.

If you attempt to live a life-style of evangelism, you will have failures. Your failures will probably outnumber your successes. You will fail because you will carry excess spiritual weight not to mention nonspiritual "encumbrances." You will fail because of doubt that Satan uses to "entangle" you. But if you will practice patience and endurance and above all else keep your eyes fixed on Jesus, you will know the assurance of victory and your chances of being an effective witness will be greatly increased. Being aware of the possibility of failures, plan on succeeding. I call that plan a personal strategy.

Continuation Through a Personal Strategy of EvangeLife

Strategy is an indispensable part of successful growth. No corporation succeeds without a long-range strategy. No athletic team leaves the field a winner that does not take the field with a strategy or game plan. No church grows much without a long-range planning committee and a workable strategy. Likewise, Christians ought to have their own strategy for life-style evangelism. Included in this strategy will be concerns, such as your own spiritual condition, the spiritual condition of non-Christians whom you know, excuses for failure to witness, areas of interest in the lives of nonbelievers you know, methods of witness which you can use, items of prayer, goals, and progress reports. Your strategy does not have to be as spectacular as that of others. I heard about a small man saying to a big man, "If I were as big as you, I'd go out in the woods and kill a big bear." The big man is reported to have replied, "Little buddy, there are a lot of little bears in the woods." For you, a strategy of "little bears" may be an acceptable goal.

Your strategy of life-style evangelism should include a process of goal setting and evaluation. Your goals should be both challenging and attainable. It will do you little good to set a goal of verbally witnessing to one person per day if you are presently witnessing to no one. Although the goal would be challenging, for practical reasons it probably would not be attainable. Begin with a goal to verbally witness to one person per week. If you are already witnessing to one person per week, you need to increase your goal to one per day to make it challenging.

Several years ago I set a goal of reading the Bible through in one year. Although I had read the Bible almost all of my life, I had never read it through in a systematic way in one year. The task was difficult. I bogged down in 2 Chronicles and got so far behind during the summer that I thought I'd never catch up. The goal was challenging because I had never done it before. The goal was attainable because I knew I could do it. The accomplishment of the goal was rewarding not only for what I gained from my reading but also for the discipline it added to my life and the feeling of success which it brought.

My next goal was to work with one passage of Scripture per week: read the passage on Monday, meditate and listen to the passage on Tuesday, study the passage on Wednesday with the assistance of commentaries, memorize the passage or at least a portion of it on Thursday, and apply the passage in some meaningful way on Friday and/or Saturday. This goal not only improved my relationship to God, it also improved my witness as I went about in my weekly responsibilities.

A part of your personal strategy of life-style evangelism will be the concept of "as you go." You are a witness in your traffic pattern, perhaps the best one somebody knows. In his Great Commission, Jesus' main imperative to his disciples was not to go, he assumed they would be going places. What else does one do with good news but share it as one goes? The option of not sharing as one goes is a rather modern one. Rather than going with the good news, we program it, protect it, and franchise it. The strategy of our Lord was to share the good news as he went about. Strong consideration should be given to your witness: as you go, where you go, when you go, why you go, and how you go. Granted, there are times when we go on purpose to share a Christian witness with a nonbeliever, but this must be balanced with the concept of witnessing "as you go," for only in this balance will the good news reach and effectively touch the entire world.

Never plan a strategy of evangelism without including the whole world. There is an "allness" to the gospel which we must not ignore, even in personal strategies. In the following passages, note the use of the word *all*. Jesus said, "And I, if I be lifted up from the earth, will draw all men to Myself " (John 12:32). He instructed his disciples to "make disciples of all the nations" (Matthew 28:19), and again, "Unless you repent, you will all likewise perish" (Luke 13:3). Jesus prayed that "all of them may be as one" (John 17:21, NIV). Paul said God did not spare his own Son, but "delivered Him up for us all" (Rom. 8:32), and Peter said God desired, "all to come to repentance" (2 Pet. 3:9).

Remember how fascinated you were the first time you threw a rock into a pond or a lake or, if you were like me, into a stock tank? Remember the excitement in watching the circles increase until they reached the edges of the body of water? You could hardly wait to throw in another rock to watch it happen again. Your witness is like that. One word, one deed, spreads from you to others, and who can say but what it will continue to spread until it reaches the ends of the earth. That has certainly been true in my experience.

Little did A. L. Gilliam know that the impact he had on my young life would someday be enlarged to national proportions. My grandfather spent his life helping people, and I watched him. Because I lived with him in my early childhood, I saw his sensitivity and his love for persons in need. His Sundays were devoted to taking me to church services of various denominations and train stations to watch the trains go through. Without knowing it, he planted in me a love for God's people wherever they meet and under whatever banner and a desire to travel. Now I travel this nation to assist and equip God's people to help others. The ripples in the pond continue.

When Pat Ankenman, a former professional baseball player, taught Sunday School to a junior boy in the South Main Baptist Church in Houston, Texas, he did not know the full impact he was making. When Ed King, railroad postal agent, taught a teenage boy in Sunday School at the West End Baptist Church in Houston and took him fishing on Saturday in Galveston Bay, he had little idea of the full impact of his labors. When Dick Turner, pharmacist, kept inviting a college ministerial student to give a devotional in his Sunday School department in the First Baptist Church of Nacogdoches, Texas, he had no concept of its impact. The list could go on to include Royal Ambassador leaders who insisted that Scripture be memorized and missionary names be learned, Church Training leaders who felt that parts on the program should be given without looking at the quarterly, and patient people who listened to early sermons and graciously complimented the effort. To all of these and more, I owe a great segment of my ministry. Where I go, they go with me. What I say has been affected by their impact on my life. Whether they had a strategy or not, I do not know. But this I know: their ministry affected me and for now at least has nationwide implications. Your influence is like that on someone. Don't ever plan a strategy of evangelism without including the world.

As you plan and implement your strategy, you will need to remember several important points. Be sensitive to nonbelievers, trying to understand their needs, their feelings, and their hurts. Remember that cultivation is sometimes slow, requiring patience, and dialogue is always two-way: two-way talk and two-way listen. Remember that knowledge is important—knowledge of God, of yourself, and of non-Christians—and openness is essential since most people can spot a cover-up. Since folk have become used to false and deceitful practices, honesty and integrity are of utmost importance. Your testimony is yours and cannot be refuted, but it ought to present Jesus in a way that cannot be refused. Remember to stay with the nonbelievers even if they seem to lose interest. Don't ever give up; anyone can quit. You're made for something higher than that. Be faithful in developing a life-style that undergirds what you say about Jesus and be faithful to verbalize your faith in a way that is consistent with your life-style. Now you're ready to work on your personal strategy of EvangeLife.

I heard that during perilous wartimes the government of the United States was discussing ways to destroy German submarines that had infiltrated the waters of the North Atlantic. When all methods seemed either too risky or too futile, Will Rogers came forth with a solution. According to Rogers, the solution was simple: just heat the water in the North Atlantic to boiling. All the Germans in the submarines would be burned up, and the problem would be solved. It sounded like a great idea, but eventually someone asked Will Rogers how to boil the water in the North Atlantic to which he replied that he had the idea; it was up to them to work out the strategy. Well, I've given you my ideas on life-style evangelism. Now it's your job to work out your strategy, and as you go, continue to evangelize.

For Further Study

Baker, Charles. *It's My World.* Nashville: Convention Press, 1980.

Coleman, Robert E. *The Master Plan of Evangelism.* Westwood, N. J.: Fleming H. Revell Co., 1963, 1964.

Douglas, J. D., editor. *Let the Earth Hear His Voice.* Minneapolis, Mn.: World Wide Publications, 1975.

Fish, Roy J. and Conant, J. E. *Every Member Evangelism for Today.* New York: Harper & Row Publishers, 1976.

Goerner, H. Cornell. *All Nations in God's Purpose.* Nashville: Broadman Press, 1979.

Hardman, Keith J. *The Spiritual Awakeners.* Chicago: Moody Press, 1983.

Hawkins, O. S. *After Revival Comes.* Nashville: Broadman Press, 1981.

Henrichsen, Walter A. *Disciples Are Made Not Born.* Wheaton, Il.: Victor Books, 1974.

Hughes, Charles L. *Goal Setting.* New York: American Management, 1965.

Johnson, Ron, Hinkle, Joseph W., and Lowry, Charles M. *Oikos: A Practical Approach to Family Evangelism.* Nashville: Broadman Press, 1982.

Neighbour, Ralph W., Jr. and Thomas, Calvin. *Target Group Evangelism.* Nashville: Broadman Press, 1975.

Olford, Stephen F. *Heart-Cry for Revival.* Westwood, N.J.: Fleming H. Revell Co., 1962.

Roselle, Charles M. *The Church's Mission to the Campus.* Nashville: Convention Press, 1969.

Scarborough, L. R., revised by E. D. Head. *With Christ After the Lost.* Nashville: Broadman Press, 1952.

Willis, Avery, Jr. *Biblical Basis of Missions.* Nashville: Convention Press, 1979.

Wood, Britton. *Single Adults Want to be the Church Too.* Nashville: Broadman Press, 1977.

Conclusion

Many words have been used in this book. Words are vehicles of thought and as such have changed lives and the course of history. I remember ten words written by William Shakespeare that not only I but thousands of school-age children had to memorize, and those words affected our lives. The ten words were: "To be, or not to be: that is the question." As a college senior, I placed a great deal of hope in nine words spoken by a newly elected president of the United States because he spoke words related to my future when John F. Kennedy said: "The torch has been passed to a new generation." Five words almost made a man a world dictator; because of those words and the determination of a nation to prove them false, my early childhood years were spent with grandparents, hearing about my father who was "overseas." Adolph Hitler's five words were: "Today Germany; tomorrow the world." I was a campus minister when four words swept this country from the west coast to the east coast and affected everything I was doing. The words represented a life-style, and we are still suffering from the affect of "do your own thing."

This book concludes with two words. Words that could change your life, your home, your church, your city, your nation, your world. These two words will make all the difference in your life-style of evangelism. Are you ready for them? Here are the two words: *Do it!* These two words are biblical. Do you remember the account of the wedding feast in Cana of Galilee during the first year of Jesus' public ministry? The host had run out of wine, and Mary had informed Jesus only to receive a gentle rebuke. She then turned to the servants and said, "Whatever He says to you, do it" (John 2:5). If I am not mistaken, Jesus has told us to evangelize the entire world as we go. DO IT!

Your commitment to DO IT is more important than how you go about doing it. It is of secondary importance which methodology you choose, for God will guide you into the "how to" of evangelizing once you commit yourself to the task and the life-style that supports it. I've saved my best illustration for last. I feel sorry for speakers and writers who don't have children. They miss some great illustrations.

When my son, James, was seven years old, he played his first year of organized baseball. That was a great summer for our family. But James was not a very good baseball player at age seven, nor were most of his teammates very good. Because James had a great difficulty throwing the baseball in the direction he wanted to throw it, the coach wisely put him in center field. Center field is a safe place for a questionable arm since most other seven-year-olds can't hit the ball that far, even with their coaches doing the pitching. About the third game of the season, with James in center field and our team ahead by one run, the opposing team got a runner on first base with two outs. Since this was the last inning, nerves were tense.

Several semimiraculous things happened in rapid succession. The seven-year-old batter somehow got the bat on the ball and sent a screaming line drive about six inches off the ground past the pitcher, over second base, and into center field. As James bent over, the ball hit his glove on one hop as the runner on first base broke for second. The ball had reached James so quickly he was momentarily confused as to what he should do. Most of the time either the right fielder or left fielder would be there to fight him for the right to throw the ball back. But no one was there, and it soon became obvious that he needed to return the ball, so he wound up and let it fly. I remember thinking about shutting my eyes, but I was too slow. The ball was on the way, and it was a perfect peg to the second baseman.

The national league all-star center fielder couldn't have made a better throw. The ball hit the second baseman in his glove and stuck. The runner from first base arrived just a split-second later and ran into the second baseman causing both seven-year-olds to fall to the ground, but somehow the baseball stayed in the glove, and the umpire yelled, "You're out!" The game was over, and we had won. James was a hero. As he ran in from center field with a newfound championship trot, his buddies were patting him where you are supposed to pat a pro who makes a good throw. The coach ran out and picked him up and awarded him the game ball. The mothers in the stands were all screaming, "Nice throw James" and "Way to go James." My son was a hero, and I was trying to act like I was not surprised.

My favorite time with James that summer was driving home after the games. I made a commitment to myself on his behalf that I would make that trip home a positive experience for him. I would not criticize, I would just affirm and help James enjoy his summer, even if his team lost and he did poorly. But this day I was at a loss for words. I wanted to be honest with my son, yet I did not want to destroy his newfound pride in himself, so I was silent for two or three blocks.

James spoke first with a question. "Dad, was that a good throw?" I couldn't remember at the time if I was supposed to bust or burst with pride, so I just did both.

All the while I was saying things like "Son, that was a great throw," and "I knew you could do it," and "I am so proud of you," James was saying in ever increasing volume, "Dad!" "Dad!" "DAD!" "DAD!"

Finally, I asked what he wanted and to my shock he said, "I was throwing it to the pitcher."

Now you need to know one rule of seven-year-old baseball to fully understand and appreciate the story. Since most seven-year-olds cannot throw the ball very far or very accurately, they are coached to just throw the ball back to the pitcher. When the ball reaches the pitcher, all the base runners have to stop. This keeps the score from being in the fifties and the game from lasting only one inning. So James was doing exactly what he had been coached to do. He was doing what he intended to do, what he desired to do, what he was committed to do, what in his heart he knew he ought to do. The result turned out far better than any of us ever dreamed.

That, my friend, is life-style evangelism. You know what you ought to do. You know what you are committed to do. DO IT, and leave the results up to God. I will almost guarantee you that the results will turn out far better than you ever dreamed. And one thing more, as you DO IT, your methodology will improve and so will your results.

"Be ye doers of the word, and not hearers only" (Jas. 1:22, KJV).

Appendix A
Personal Strategy
for EvangeLife

NONBELIEVERS THAT YOU KNOW: List below the names of several non-believers that you know personally. This will help you to focus on specific persons in this strategy.

_____

_____

_____

_____

SPIRITUAL CONDITION OF SELF: What is your present relationship to God through his Word, the Bible? How about your relationship to God through worship and service? To what degree are you experiencing the power of the Holy Spirit in your life? What adjustments are needed? You may need to review chapters 2 and 3 for assistance with these questions.

SPIRITUAL CONDITION OF NONBELIEVERS: List some of the needs of your non-Christian friends. What, if any, indications of conviction do you see in their lives? You may need to review chapter 4 for assistance with these questions.

BARRIERS TO WITNESS: Make a list of the problems you are having with your witnessing. What excuses do you offer for not verbalizing your faith in a greater way? What seems to be Satan's strategy for preventing you from being a better witness? You may want to review chapter 6 for assistance with these questions.

NONBELIEVERS' AREAS OF INTEREST: Determine how and where to begin a conversation with your non-Christian friends. What kind of ministry could you perform in their lives? How could you meet some of their needs? You may want to review chapters 4 and 5 for assistance with these questions.

AREAS OF TRANSITION IN WITNESS ENCOUNTER: Determine how to move from general conversation to specific witness. What general conversations will lead to smooth transition? How can you get your non-Christian friends to discuss these matters? You may want to review chapters 6 and 7 for assistance with these questions.

METHODS USED IN WITNESSING: Consider which methods or approaches will be acceptable to your non-Christian friends. Which Scripture verses would be appropriate? Is there a tract that speaks to their needs? What would be the advantage of using a New Testament to show them the plan of salvation? Will your testimony apply to their needs, if so, which parts? How can you use your spiritual gifts related to their needs? What are some good questions to ask to make them think? You may want to review chapters 6 and 7 for assistance with these questions.

ITEMS OF PRAYER: Make a prayer list of needs in the lives of your non-Christian friends for which you could pray. You may want to review chapter 5 for assistance with this strategy.

NAME _____   NAME _____   NAME _____
_____   _____   _____
_____   _____   _____
_____   _____   _____
_____   _____   _____

GOALS: Set several challenging, yet attainable goals for yourself. You may want to review chapter 8 for assistance with this strategy.

_____
_____
_____
_____

PROGRESS REPORT/FOLLOW THROUGH: Evaluate your strategy from time to time. You may need to reset your goals or adjust your strategy.

Appendix B
Group Strategy
for EvangeLife

CREATE AN ATMOSPHERE AND MIND-SET THAT IS CONDUCIVE TO EVANGELISM: What kind of motivational methods can you use in your group to encourage evangelism? In what ways can you make evangelism a part of everything your group does? How can evangelism become the "in thing" with your group? You may want to consider hosting an EvangeLife seminar as a motivational tool for group evangelism.

EQUIP CHRISTIANS TO EVANGELIZE NON-CHRISTIANS: What training methods would be best suited for your group? Consider both a "crash-course" training method and a continual training method. In Appendix C, there are several suggestions for further training.

ENCOURAGE VERBAL, LIFE-STYLE WITNESSING AMONG CHRIS-TIANS: What kind of continual, consistent encouragement can be offered to your group? In what ways can the leaders set the pace for group involvement? How can you keep the methods learned in the training sessions alive when the initial momentium wears off?

ATTEMPT OCCASIONAL MASS EVANGELISM PROGRAMS FOR THE PURPOSE OF EVANGELIZING NON-CHRISTIANS: What type of mass methods would be best for your group? What personalities should be invited to share in this effort or would your own people be the best leaders? When is the best time to have such a mass effort, and where is the best location? How will the follow-up be done so new Christians are not left without guidance?

DEMAND EFFECTIVE FOLLOW-UP OF NEW AND YOUNG CHRIS-
TIANS: What materials will you use in discipling new Christians? Who will do
this follow-up? How long will the follow-up last? What will be taught to new
Christians that will make them effective witnesses and a valuable part of your
group?

Appendix C
For Further
Training and Growth

For most persons, further training in evangelism is not only necessary but desirable. The following training methods are recommended.

From the Personal Evangelism Department, Home Mission Board, SBC, 1350 Spring Street, NW, Atlanta, Georgia 30367-5601:

The Lay Evangelism School (LES): The Lay Evangelism School involves the learner in a group study of the basics of "how to witness." Persons are won to Christ while others are being trained to witness. The Lay Evangelism School involves a three-month preparation period, one week of intensive training, and three months of continued training.

TELL Witness Training (TELL): Training for Evangelistic Life-style Leadership can be used in any size group or individually. Through the use of a LaBelle Duo 16 projector and specially prepared cartridges, training is offered in life-style evangelism. By purchasing the TELL equipment from the Home Mission Board, the local group is free to set its own schedule for this training. There are twelve sessions of sixty minutes each.

Continuing Witness Training (CWT): Continuing Witness Training is a continuous process for training personal witnesses. Apprentices who complete the initial thirteen-week training cycle and memorize the Model Presentation and principles become equippers of others. Using a memorized presentation of the gospel, CWT involves the participants in the disciplines of intercessory prayer, systematic Bible study, Scripture memorization, personal witnessing, and follow-up.

From National Student Ministries, The Sunday School Board, 127 Ninth Avenue, North, Nashville, Tennessee, 37234:

Share Seminar: This basic training in Christian growth and witness is designed for use in a group study directed by a trained leader. The seminar helps you be certain of your own relationship with Christ, assists you in discovering where you are in your Christian life as you move toward full maturity in Christ, builds solid scriptural principles into your life for Christian growth and witness, and teaches skills for getting to know people by being sensitive to their needs and responding through ministry and verbal witness.

From the Specialized Evangelism Department, Home Mission Board, SBC, 1350 Spring Street, NW, Atlanta, Georgia 30367-5601:

EvangeLife: A Seminar in Life-style Evangelism: This seminar is based on the outline contained in this book. Small group interaction times follow each chapter/ session. This seminar comes in three editions: College Adult Edition, Single Adult Edition, and Married Adult Edition.